wanted to be respectful of his dad, and all of the families, friends, and the many other people who have influenced our lives in one way or another. In the interest of privacy, I have either changed the names of or omitted altogether important people in our lives who requested they not be mentioned on paper.

I have laughed a lot, cried a lot, reflected a lot, and occasionally gotten really pissed off. No one has the perfect life. But making your life as perfect as it can be for you is the challenge. For me, it was about embracing my authentic self and letting go of the need to pretend to be anyone else. That took some doing.

We all have the same rights to be respected, to be loved, and to live with dignity. To me, this a story of optimism over defeat, of courage over despair, of love over grief, and of everything in between.

I hope you enjoy it.

# 1

# The Opposite of Up

"Babies are bits of stardust blown from the
hand of God. Lucky the woman who knows the
pangs of birth for she has held a star."
—LARRY BARRETTO

We had only recently settled into our new home when I learned that
I was pregnant. It was shortly after my thirtieth birthday, and I was
taken quite by surprise, as was my husband, Graeme. I had never given
pregnancy or motherhood much thought. I assumed that I'd focus on
my career and that Graeme, who was working from our new home,
would renovate the house, and we would get our lives in order and
then have a baby—*maybe*. Graeme was thirty-four and we had been
together, on and off, for ten years. They had not all been great years,
but when we finally married in 1988, we knew that the next phase
of our life needed to come with a change. Two years later we made
the move to our new home with a renewed commitment to our life
together.

Our old home had been in Marrickville, which was, at that time,
about as multicultural as you could get. An inner-Sydney working-
class area, Marrickville was full of Greeks, Italians, Vietnamese, and
a whole lot more. With my Maltese background I fit right in; with
Graeme's Anglo-Saxon background he wasn't so comfortable. At least
he had dark hair. If you ever saw anyone with blond hair and blue

eyes in Marrickville, you could safely assume they were lost. I loved it there. I loved the food, the crazy drivers, the hint of crime and mayhem that was round each and every corner. But our home was small, and Graeme wanted to head back to his more conservative roots.

Sydney's Upper North Shore was the complete opposite to Marrickville, and I did not fit in. If you ever saw anyone on the Upper North Shore with dark hair and dark skin and who was especially loud, you could safely assume they were lost. Massive trees, beautiful manicured gardens, birds, and nature were in abundance. Well-tended paths were about the only thing that had concrete. Graeme was right at home. I gave myself over to the idea that I could do this, that it would be a new beginning, but I didn't like that our new home was a long way from the city and my family.

Our new home in Mount Colah was very sweet but needed a lot of work. It had once housed a family of four boys, and their imprint was still there on doorways and walls. The mother of the boys was a gardener, and both Graeme and I loved that our new home had a well-established if somewhat out-of-control jungle of a garden. The backyard was barely visible under a massive kiwi vine that encroached on all aspects of the yard. Somewhere out there was a clothesline, some fruit trees, and a rickety shed.

The house was weatherboard, with charming French windows and doors, but it had the ugliest carpet you've ever laid eyes on. Originally a small two-bedroom cottage, the previous family had extended it to house all those boys, and it was now a four-bedroom, two-bathroom home. It seemed like a palace to me—so much space—but it was much too quiet. I was sure if I sneezed, the whole street would hear me. In Marrickville you could hardly hear the doorbell ring with the sound of the traffic and the planes overhead landing at the nearby international airport. I thought I would go deaf from the suburban silence.

This new environment seemed so conservative, so middle-class, so—dare I say it?—*Australian*. I had never before lived in a community where the local deli sold only mortadella, cocktail sausages, and Spam, and even garlic was seen as something exotic. Now, in the local shopping center, I was perhaps the only Mediterranean. What had I done in moving there?

There was no possible answer; I simply had to embrace the unknown.

❧

When I became pregnant, I was working at the ABC (Australian Broadcasting Corporation). It was my dream job with my dream team of people. The ABC had opened a number of retail outlets, and I worked in the book-buying division. Each day was full of new books, new ideas, new people. Graeme wasn't thrilled by how many hours I worked, but I couldn't get enough of the excitement and energy of it all. It was a truly dynamic place to work, so it was with some sadness that I requested my maternity leave.

By the time my due date neared, my stomach was huge. My niece, Faith, called me "Big Ben." An ultrasound had indicated we were having a boy, and the name Richard had been decided upon very early in the pregnancy. I would have preferred Sam, but Graeme was adamant it had to be Richard, his own middle name. I had nightmares my son would be called Dick. I also had some girls' names tucked away, just in case.

I'd decided I didn't want genetic testing. I was active, healthy, and at my age not considered high-risk. My blood tests came back with no markers for any abnormalities. The only sign something might be amiss was an ultrasound when I was eighteen weeks pregnant, showing that the baby's arms and legs were at the developmental stage of a sixteen-week pregnancy. I asked the obstetrician why this was. He was very cagey with me but gave me no reason to think there was anything serious we needed to discuss.

No matter. I would love my child regardless. And anyway, Richard was going to fly high. I couldn't decide whether he would be the next David Attenborough, a brilliant actor like Robert De Niro, or a writer—yes, a writer to follow my passion for literature. Or maybe a talented painter. It was so exciting to think that anything was possible for this little person. I dreamed big.

It had never ever occurred to me that I would have anything but the perfect baby. This baby would grow to be a devilishly cute toddler, a child who would be the most loved student in primary school. My son, my Richard, would power his way through the most exclusive private boys' school, captain the football team, and lead a successful debating team. Other parents would be in awe of my parenting skills and the solidarity of our family unit. (His siblings being equally blessed.) At his final-year speech night, he would thank his parents for all the support, opportunities, and love we had given him. He would choose either Harvard or Cambridge, and I would visit him often. Neither Graeme nor I had a university degree, something I always regretted. Graeme was much more laid-back about such things than I was. I was always the one who wanted more. I wanted more than I had for my child.

My capacity for daydreaming during my pregnancy was limitless. I once completely missed my train stop, so immersed was I in this fantasy land. These daydreams reassured me the future would be nothing short of brilliant.

One day, lost in daydreams while shopping, I saw a very attractive woman, beautifully dressed and coiffured (unlike me in my enormous maternity ensemble, which included, appropriately and embarrassingly, an elephant-printed pantsuit) coming toward me on the up escalator as I was heading downward. She was chatting to a teenage girl in a private school uniform. Mother and daughter. The daughter I recognized as having Down syndrome.

In that moment, there was a sudden kick in my belly, then another and another, and then a roar of thunder from outside and an almighty bang. An unexpected cyclone had suddenly hit Sydney's northern suburbs. Roofs were torn away, power lines came down, and cars crashed on the freeways. Everywhere I turned, there was chaos. I looked back at the woman, and she smiled at me as we both held on to the escalator for fear of another thunderbolt. I smiled at her daughter. She didn't smile back but shyly held her mother's hand. The kicks from within returned, giving me a start. My hand instinctively clutched my belly. The building shook once more as I approached the car park, thinking still of that mother and daughter. Black clouds covered the sun and then the heavens opened.

⤚

It's funny how you remember the most innocuous things when your life is about to change irrevocably. Graeme had just put the first coat of varnish on our newly sanded floorboards when my waters broke.

"What? Now? He's not due for another two weeks."

"Well, I can't help it. Your son wants to come out . . . now!"

We both laughed. On the drive to the hospital, I was a little apprehensive about the imminent birth of the little person demanding to come into the world, so I took some comfort from Matt Monro and his golden tonsils, soothing me with "Born Free." I was thinking about those little orphaned lion cubs from the 1966 film and how cute and cuddly they were. *Born free, as free as the wind blows.* I wondered if I was going to have a child with a golden mane and a rambunctious personality, and whether he or she might be a little quirky in a delightful sort of way. Neither Graeme nor I appeared to carry a blond gene, so I have no idea why I thought that. We were, however, both a little quirky. Although he had been a public servant for many years, Graeme was really creative. An excellent artist, writer, and quite the handyman and gardener, he was also hugely passionate about steam trains. His fledgling home business was making videos about steam trains. My passion was books: I had worked in bookshops and publishing houses for most of my working life, and loved nothing more than spending hours reading the latest bestseller. And I, too, loved the garden. The joy it brings fills your heart. I couldn't wait to sit with my little baby in our backyard just dreaming away the days.

At the hospital, pulled back to my present reality, I was not at all happy with my extreme state of discomfort. As we waited patiently with a roomful of other pregnant couples, it suddenly occurred to me that perhaps something was not quite right. "Why are the other women about to give birth looking so relaxed? I am in excruciating pain," I asked.

Worry passed over Graeme's face until he offered brightly, "They must be here for the tour of the labor ward." Again we laughed.

Finally, a pinched-faced midwife arrived and ushered us into a room and looked at me very strangely. I wondered if perhaps, once again, I looked ridiculous in my elephant-patterned maternity outfit. A poor fashion choice, indeed. The nurse stuck a monitor onto my bulging tummy. Heartbeat strong. We were doing fine. Excellent. She was now on Team Richard. Yes! Not only did I want the perfect child, I also wanted the perfect labor.

Time is relative when you are about to give birth to something the size of a watermelon. The amount of time I'd spent in extreme discomfort meant my plans for a drug-free birth were now completely blown out of the water. I found myself screaming at the midwife and Graeme. I even screamed at the cleaner. "Give me the pethidine—now! Hurry up!"

The drugs worked, and everyone calmed. At 9:01 a.m. on Friday, March 22, 1991, Richard Phillip Charles was born.

It happened so fast that both Graeme and the obstetrician missed the birth, and I was instead attended by two midwives. Graeme had ducked home for a bit of rest, and was later bewildered that he had slept through the whole thing. Not ideal, but the important thing was we now had a beautiful baby boy.

When Richard arrived, the midwives took a long time inspecting him. Although we were 90 percent sure it was a boy, I still asked the question "Is it a girl or a boy?" several times over but got no answer.

It was then I started to panic.

"Give me my baby," I said.

Finally, as he lay resting on my breast, I looked at my tiny little baby and felt the deepest love. Suddenly nothing else mattered. I heard nothing; I was completely focused on this little person who had already stolen my heart. I can still smell him: his newness, his soul, and his breath. What a true blessing it is to be part of that amazing entry into the world. I was in a vacuum of calm and surrender.

"Bernadette, we have to take your baby away and put him under the sunlamp, as he is a little jaundiced."

"Oh, sorry. What? Oh, yes, he does look a little suntanned," I replied.

I checked off his fingers and toes and, of course, double-checked that he really was a boy. I inhaled him a few more times and handed him over to the midwife. Having given up on trying to find my sleeping husband, I started calling other members of the family. The room echoed with the news we'd had a boy—not just a boy, but the most beautiful boy ever, I swore. I don't think in my whole life I had ever felt that euphoric. I sat in bed feeling smug and clever. Three pushes and he was out. He was tiny, sweet, and scrunchy, and he was mine.

Graeme finally awoke and made his way to the room, but Richard was, by now, elsewhere. He was understandably anxious to meet his son. I buzzed the midwife and again an age went past before the delivery room doors finally parted. When I think about that moment, I remember vividly the white light streaming through the windows and the blueness of the sky. I loved those clear Sydney days and always felt happy to be alive on them. There is a calm about that blue.

When the doors opened, they revealed an army of people in white coats accompanied by my two midwives. The looks on their faces caused my heart to skip a beat. The number of medical staff coming into the room now made me anxious. What was wrong? Where was my son? *Oh, God, don't tell me he's dead. Not my beautiful, precious boy.*

I couldn't breathe. I couldn't speak. I could feel my heart beating so fast and hard, it was deafening. Panic swirled over me in waves. A woman who resembled a humbler version of Morticia Addams from *The Addams Family* approached the bed. I was sitting upright, and Graeme was in a chair next to me. She finally spoke.

"Hello, I'm Dr. Sandra Grass, and I am one of the hospital pediatricians. I have with me a team of interns . . ."

At this point I had stopped listening, stopped paying attention, and was hoping that Graeme would just take all of them away and go find our baby. I was now convinced our baby had died, and I just wanted to be anywhere but in the hospital. Dr. Grass looked at me, paused, and then spoke.

"We believe that your baby has Down syndrome."

*Thank you, God, thank you, God. He lives. He is alive.*

"Oh, thank God," I said. "Is that all? I thought you were going to tell me he'd died."

The room became brighter and Dr. Grass laughed. Graeme, however, began to look gray, the blood slowly draining from his face.

"What does that mean?"

I could hear the fear in his voice.

"Well, he has this extra chromosome that will make him a little slow."

Without any warning, I buckled. I was exhausted, and I came crashing down. I just wanted my baby. That love, that bond, was growing by the minute, and I just wanted to hold him. I was told that the reason for the delay was because the midwives had been uncertain about whether Richard had Down syndrome, as he did not present with all the features. They had not yet met Graeme, and they wondered if my son's father might be Asian: Richard had the sweetest almond-shaped eyes, which is one of the indicators of Down syndrome. Other features of the syndrome include a fold at the back of the neck, a flatter face (especially the nose), little fingers, a crease across the palm of the hand, and a protruding tongue. Some babies have all of these and some only have a few. The other biggie is weak muscle tone in the baby, and Richard had loads of that.

To add to the mix there are three types of Down syndrome. There is your run-of-the-mill trisomy 21, which basically means you are born with an extra chromosome. So instead of forty-six like most people, people with Down syndrome have forty-seven; they have three of the very unsuspecting twenty-first chromosome. A total of 95 percent of people with Down syndrome fall into this group. That's why they have that physical sameness about them. The other two types—translocation and mosaicism—make up the other 5 percent and they are rare, as the chromosomes do very odd things. With translocation, which 4 percent of people with Down syndrome have, the twenty-first chromosome breaks off and jumps onto the fourteenth chromosome. It's so strange to think that all these little parts of cells are just having a bit of fun trying out something new and yet can have hugely significant effects on the baby. More bizarrely, with mosaicism (which represents the remaining 1 percent), some cells have forty-six chromosomes and others have forty-seven, meaning these babies with Down syndrome function at a much higher level than the rest.

I knew none of this when those words "Down syndrome" were mentioned. I just knew at that moment that it wasn't good news; in fact, it was devastating news.

Once the doctor gave her diagnosis, the midwives finished up the cleaning and swaddling of our newborn, and eventually he was delivered back to me.

The white coats finally left and new phones calls had to be made. The words stuck in my throat. Down syndrome. Although I was relieved that Richard was alive, I was now returning to reality. What did this Down syndrome mean? This was not what I wanted; this was not the future I had so happily daydreamed about.

Tests had to be done to ensure the diagnosis was correct, and although Richard looked a little like my auntie Doris, I remembered the girl on the escalators with her funny little face. I knew there was no need to conduct the tests. He had the signs, but I was probably hoping he had the rarer mosaicism form of Down syndrome. I said more than a few Hail Marys, but when the test did return some weeks later, it showed he had standard trisomy 21 Down syndrome.

In a weird, reassuring way it came upon me that I was always meant to have this child. Although I was struggling to process everything that was happening, I started thinking about what we needed to do. The hospital staff was supportive and kind. My obstetrician, who had turned up only to stitch me up and disappeared again, dropped by to see me.

"Congratulations on your son," he said. His warmth was genuine. "I know this will be very hard, but I also know you can do this. Take him home and love him as much as you can. It will be all right."

I thought that was pretty good advice. All you need is love. But it turned out we would need a whole lot more.

The first of my family to arrive at the hospital were my sister Martha and my mother. Martha came with champagne, balloons, and an attitude that said, "We're not going to let this define him." My mother picked up Richard and announced he was perfect and a gift from God. She then turned to me.

"You look terrible. Put some lipstick on!"

Mum and I are poles apart when it comes to grooming and fashion. She was still a young woman when she immigrated from Malta; she was twenty-seven years old and had three girls under six. Mum never looks anything other than fabulous. With her hair, nails, makeup, and matching shoes and handbag, she has a real sense of style. Always the fashionista, she expected her daughters to be the same. I, however, was never one for high street fashion. As a teenager, I chose thrift shops for my clothes. I was happy in black: gender neutral and cheap. As an adult, other than my maternity indiscretions, I still dressed in black; the only real change was buying from well-known brands. I rarely bothered with things like manicures, makeup, or facials, but always had excellent hair and dyed it all sorts of colors. Now I found myself propped up in bed, feeling like crap, and apparently looking like it, too, as I pondered the enormity of having a child with Down syndrome. A makeover, in more ways than one, would be in order.

*I should look like that woman on the escalator,* I told myself, *so that I will look normal even if my child doesn't. I should start buying bright clothes and have my hair cut in a bob and wear the best designer labels so that I fit in, and that will make Richard fit in.*

My mind was going round and round, and somewhere in all of this I still had to become a breast-feeding, diaper-changing mum. I needed to have mum-like thoughts. *Is he breathing? Has he soiled his diaper? Is he too cold? Or too hot? Is he attaching properly when I feed him? Should I buy one of those baby monitor things?*

Graeme's parents had no other grandchildren, unlike mine, who had three granddaughters already. For my in-laws, Richard's birth was full of anticipation and expectation. They were so excited. Like me, Graeme, and just about everyone, they were shocked with the uncertainty of the future, but the day our baby was born was nonetheless a day of celebration. Richard was welcomed into the world with excitement.

⌇

Graeme had never been exposed to anyone with an intellectual disability. Later he admitted he'd always wondered why some people with an intellectual disability had a sameness about their appearance. He had no experience to help him understand what this meant for his child.

My exposure to intellectual disabilities began early in life. When I was a young girl, my mother had our best dresses made by a fabulous dressmaker named Josephine. Everyone wanted their dresses made by Josephine, although I was more curious about the whiskers growing out of her chin (and there were many) than her dressmaking skills. Going to get a fitting from Josephine also meant being tortured by Pauline, her daughter, who would scream at me, looked very odd, and didn't speak. We just knew she was not like the rest of us. To my mother's credit she would make my sisters and me play with Pauline, and we had to be nice to her. If we pulled faces or were mean to Pauline, we would be punished when we got home. Mum told us Pauline was disabled and had Down syndrome. I didn't know what that meant. To me, it just meant Pauline was an annoying pain in the butt and I had to play with her. She did make me laugh a lot, though. Eventually, I came to understand her.

When I told Cathy, my best friend from school, that Rich had Down syndrome, she responded with "So?" "So" is such a good word: it challenges one to focus on what's important. So, what does it mean not to have the "perfect" child? What is this Down syndrome thing?

Even before we left the hospital, I had a visit from two women, Suzanne and Carla, from Down Syndrome New South Wales. They lived nearby and were both mothers of little boys with Down syndrome. Part of me didn't want to see them at all; it was all too soon. *Give me more time,* I thought. *I've got to get my head around all this.*

But it turned out to be a worthwhile visit that provided me with a lot of information I needed and went on to answer some, though not all, of my questions. They told me about early intervention programs, health issues that might or might not arise, people's attitudes. But the one question that I asked was "What will he be like as an adult?" I was asking if he'd able to function fully in this world. The million-dollar question with no answer.

Both women were lovely. They talked about the "new village," most of which went over my head, but it appeared that they, too, had had to work out this unknown world of disability when their boys were born. Soon after that, I had a visit from a social worker. She told me she'd come to my home for another visit soon. I lay back on my bed trying to sort it all out in my head. *I can do this. I can do this. I can. Just breathe. In, out. In, out. Yes, I can.*

Down syndrome. In those first days in the hospital I learned a lot, very fast. Some of it made me truly sad, a sadness I had never felt before. It was like having my light and soul sucked out of me, like those Dementors in *Harry Potter* do. I also learned that there was hope, that there was light, and it wasn't the end of the world. I also learned about the physical difference of a child with Down syndrome. The capacity for learning was one thing, but the big red light came on with the news that life expectancy for people with Down syndrome was not good, with thirty being the average expiration date. That just about killed me. I could not get my head around this at all.

I would outlive my son. How could that be?

I had nightmares about outliving him. But then I started thinking, in my madness, that this was actually a good thing. If I outlived Richard, then I wouldn't have to worry about who would look after and care for him when I died. If I outlived him, no one could hurt him; I would always be there to protect my innocent, vulnerable little boy. Insane thinking, I know, but I was so scared.

There was also the news that children with Down syndrome have a higher rate of leukemia, vision impairments, hearing issues, holes in their hearts, thyroid problems, stomach issues . . . Oh, for God's sake, this was all just too much. He looked so sweet and gorgeous; how could all this risk be hiding inside his DNA?

Although I knew all the health concerns were really important, I wanted to know more about what would be happening to him emotionally as he grew. Could he feel joy and love? Would he understand good from bad? Could he love me? Could he love *anyone*? Would he feel hurt, hope, happiness? Could he have a sense of humor? I wanted so much for him to have "normal" human emotions. I had no idea what Down syndrome emotions would be like, and no one could really tell me. There is a uniqueness in all of us, but I wasn't sure that if you had Down syndrome you would have your own personality outside of that.

There was also potential. There was the capacity to learn, there was the possibility of speech, comprehension. Reading and writing were achievable, albeit at a slower pace. I held on to the positive possibilities, but the negative ones made me sick and anxious. I was exhausted. But there was a quiet optimistic voice in my head trying very hard to keep me sane. Sometimes it worked, sometimes it didn't, but I put on my best face whenever we had visitors come to see the newborn Richard.

As I first sat in the hospital thinking about what this all meant, I made a pact with God. Or rather, it wasn't so much a pact; it was more of an ultimatum.

Okay, God, here's the deal. I will always keep going to church, I promise, but you have to make sure that Richard can do the following:

One: He has to be able to speak to me. I want to know who he is, what he thinks, what he needs, and what he loves. I want to hear his jokes.

Two: I want him to be able to read. Words are everything; to be able to read is to succeed. I want him to know how to get to places, to know how to work, and to understand what is going on around him.

Three: And, God, this one is for me. Please let him be able to wipe his own bum in later childhood. Doing this for him as he matures would be the pits for me.

That's all I want you to do. The rest I can look after.

When my twelve-year-old niece, Carly, and her younger sister, Melanie, found out that we'd had a boy with Down syndrome, Carly didn't understand.

"What's Down syndrome?" she asked.

"It means he doesn't have enough Up syndrome," said Melanie.

Up, down, or sideways, the girls were besotted with Richard from the moment they laid eyes on him. At the same time, wise little sages that they were, they could see why everyone was both happy and anxious all at once.

"I'm going to love my way through this," Carly said.

*Yes,* I thought. *We're going to love our way through this. That's what we we're going to do.*

# 2

# Bringing Home Baby

"Life is about change. Sometimes it's painful. Sometimes it's beautiful. But most of the time, it's both."

—LANA LANG, *SMALLVILLE*

The daydreams had vanished.

My son wasn't going to set the world on fire with his brilliance and good looks and I wasn't going to be the envy of the world. Nope. None of that was going to happen.

Driving home with this tiny, sweet little boy, I had an overwhelming feeling of failure for him, for Graeme, and for both our families. It sat right in the pit of my stomach. Despite my tendency to be a Pollyanna, I couldn't conjure up the promise of hope. I felt dead in the water. But I hid it well, always smiling, always okay. On that day, driving home, the sun was bright and, as on the day Richard was born, the sky was a magnificent blue. As we drove past the park, with its swings and slides, I saw a mum and her children having fun. She looked so content. Would I ever be that content? I suddenly saw Richard as a little fellow racing toward the swings with our dog, Comet, right behind him. Perhaps I could be that content. Perhaps we would just do the baby thing first and the Down syndrome thing later. There was such a truckload of Down syndrome stuff that I found it quite overwhelming.

In hospital I was given so much information about all the special considerations we had to make—early intervention programs, endless health checks, speech pathology, physiotherapy, breast-feeding checks—I just wanted to get on with a normal life, but my life was never going to be normal again. It seemed like every waking moment would have us in Down Syndrome Land.

I was relieved to get home. I wanted to close the door behind me and leave all that Down syndrome drama outside. Graeme had made such an effort to get our home ready. The floor was finished and Richard's room was all set up: freshly painted in a warm yellow, his little crib made up with fresh linen and all the gifts from family and friends neatly placed in various parts of the room. I had never seen so many stuffed toys. I felt safer in the comfort of my home. But my mind kept circling around the same questions. Would Richard be okay? What would our lives be like?

Guilt and recrimination are a part of motherhood. It goes with the territory. Mothers who don't have children with a disability experience it, too, so how much harder is it when your child is born with a genetic abnormality? I went through the *Was it because . . . ?* stage, as all mothers do. Was it because I used to enjoy a line of speed at dance parties? Drank too much at times? Partied too hard? All those different boyfriends? Was it my diet? My age? Something I ate while pregnant? I was raised a Catholic, so guilt and I were on very familiar terms. I spent hours agonizing over whether I was being punished. Other people had partied just as hard as I had, and their children didn't have Down syndrome or anything else, so what had gone wrong? The questions swirled around in my head, but there was one question that loomed larger than the rest: Will he have a normal life?

I wondered what might have happened if I had gotten pregnant at a different time in my life. Would the outcome have been the same? Long hours were spent trying to find a medical answer, but I couldn't find anything. It was just the way it was. Statistically, at my age of thirty-one, I had a 1 in 831 chance of having a child with Down syndrome. I wish I could have those odds for a Lotto draw instead.

It can happen to anyone. It is simply a malfunction, or "an improper chromosome division," which has no rhyme or reason, and the only real reason there is more risk as you get older is because your eggs are older. It's not bad enough that everything on the outside starts sagging, but apparently on the inside it does too! But, really, thirty-one! That hardly seemed fair.

Catholic guilt morphed into motherly guilt, and from that into esoteric thinking. For a long while I bought into a particular notion about reincarnation, that this was Richard's last time on Earth and that is why he came to us as a child with Down syndrome. I clung on to that idea. It comforted me to envision him living before as a regular Joe. I went to clairvoyants, tarot readers, gurus, and spiritual healers to find out why I'd had Richard. Why was he given to *me*? One clairvoyant told me that Richard would be safe, that he would do well, and that he had been given to me because I was joyful. I liked that. The tarot cards told me to watch his health, which of course sent me into a total spin. The cards never told me why.

What I learned over time was that no amount of spirit guides, rock therapy, crystal ball gazing, chanting, or past life readings would change the fact that Richard was my son; he had my genes and his father's genes, if slightly in excess by one chromosome. Nothing would reverse who he was—past lives or not. I had to stop going to these people and abandon the quest to find out why. It was pointless (and expensive) and we'll never know the answers. But after the *Was it because . . . ?* stage and the *Why me?* stage, there were yet more stages to face.

"It takes a village to raise a child," or so the proverb goes. When you have a child with a disability, that village isn't just made up of family and friends and work colleagues. It must also include a lot of unfamiliar faces, expanding to meet all those extra needs: disability professionals, health care workers, and therapists, who all speak with words completely unknown to you. They each speak their own language and I must admit that I felt like a total dummy, completely out of my depth. All I had ever truly known was books and publishing. Fine motor skills, gross motor skills, heart murmurs, flexion furrows, visual skills, auditory skills, understanding object permanence . . . on and on it went. I was a basket case trying to keep up with it all: not only did I have a child with Down syndrome, I was also a new mother adjusting to the typical postpartum state of mind of *I lost my memory when I lost my placenta.*

We were lucky in that Richard's health was good. He was robust— well, as much as he could be for a little person who had not long been in the world. He had a small hole in his heart, which was to be monitored, but everything, for the time being, was pretty good.

As scary as it all was, Carla, the representative from Down Syndrome Association NSW, helped put it into perspective:

When you give birth to a baby with Down syndrome, you go through a grieving process. You grieve for the baby you were expecting: healthy, non-disabled. However, you soon grow to love your real baby and realize he is not so different from other babies. He will just take longer to learn things and need more support, but different is okay. Over the years of teaching your son, you also learn a lot from him. You meet some amazing people, form some great friendships, and come to realize that being a parent to a child with Down syndrome is the same as being a parent of any child. The only difference is that you know the challenges that lay ahead and are better prepared for them.

I certainly was not the maternal type and had been quite shocked when I found out I was pregnant. Having never been one of those women who like to coo over and cuddle with other people's babies, I never imagined myself as a natural mum. Now that Richard was there, I was getting quite anxious about my capacity to do the job. I knew I loved my little baby; that was never in question. The question was how I could make our lives as good as possible with what we had. How would we do this? How would we set the benchmark for everyone else?

I was so determined that he would succeed that I put his name down at a mainstream private boys' school. My son would experience the best education. I wasn't going to let a disability get in the way. I had his name down before he could even say "Mum."

I became an acolyte of the *I'm fine, we are good, it changes nothing* school of thought. And, dare I say it, even joined the *God only gives you what you can handle* brigade. I maintained that mind-set for some time, but it was more about keeping myself safe and holding it together than actually believing the mantra. Holding that belief kept reality at bay and enabled me to still trust God. That relationship, however, was starting to become fractured. Despite this, I managed to put on my happy face, my determined super-mum face.

Carla and Suzanne had told me about a world-class early intervention program at Macquarie University in Sydney that only took a few children per year. That was not going to stop me. If I couldn't have the regular kid who would set the world on fire, I was determined to have the Down syndrome kid who would achieve that.

I drove people crazy ensuring he got into the Macquarie program. Called Small Steps, the program was groundbreaking, and there was very little else on offer. The program was based on an existing program out of Seattle in the United States and was a game changer for education in Australia. The results were definitive: children with Down syndrome could and did learn literacy and numeracy, albeit at a slower rate and using different methods. The program basically worked on the premise that the more you do, the more you will achieve. But the key lay in what you did, and that was their specialty. I was desperate to get in.

Before Moira Pieterse, the program's director, and the Macquarie program, it was widely accepted in the Australian education and medical sectors that people with Down syndrome could not be educated. In Moira's own words:

I'd been asked to speak at a postgraduate seminar on Down syndrome at University of New South Wales. Lejeune, the Frenchman who identified the genetic component of Down syndrome, was the keynote speaker, so the university was holding a daylong seminar on "mongolism." I was standing behind a tall gentleman and I heard him say to his colleague, in a very English sort of voice, "I've got to introduce this woman, ha, who thinks she can teach these kids, ha ha ha!" and they both chortled away. And I thought, *He's talking about me.*

Eventually a baby, preschooler, child, or adult with Down syndrome can learn all the common skills non-disabled people learn, but it may happen at a much slower pace, and efforts to teach them may not always be successful. So, yes, Richard would walk, but to get him to walk well and within the normally accepted time frame meant we had to coax him into moving. Honestly, the poor kid was never allowed to sit still without me moving his legs from pillar to post. I used to sing "*The wheels of the bus go round and round*" while stretching his legs in circular motions. There were hours and hours of opening clothespins, of getting him to pick up little sultanas, all so that his fine motor skills would develop and hopefully one day he'd be able to do up his buttons or hold a pencil. "Graduates" from the Macquarie Down syndrome program also had a better success rate of getting into a mainstream school; for me, this was the kicker. Both Suzanne's and Carla's boys went there, so Richard had to go there too!

I must have called Moira Pieterse's office a hundred times before I finally got her on the phone. Moira was the guru of early intervention for families of babies and toddlers with Down syndrome. She had developed a world-class program and also trained student teachers in special education. The program was so significant that master's students and undergraduates queued to study under Moira and her team as part of their education degrees. Excited that I had an opportunity to give Richard the best possible start ever, I put on my "very serious professional" voice for our conversation.

"Hello, Moira. My name is Bernadette and my son Richard is a week old and has Down syndrome."

"Well, you haven't wasted any time."

"No, I haven't. I know it's early days, but I really want Richard to join your program."

I have no idea what her reply was, nor any idea what I said in return, but I do know that I was sobbing loudly when I heard her say, "Bring him in six weeks; we can start then. Enjoy your new baby."

We were in. Woo-hoo! I put the phone down, found Graeme, and told him the news. He cried. I cried. I felt that for now we had been rescued. We didn't have to do this all alone; help was at hand. I tucked that into my "lucky break" folder and took the attitude that from here on in we could control the agenda.

❧

The first few months of Richard's life—with all their uncertainty and adjustment—started to change my outlook. There was so much to do. I was on six months' maternity leave, but I wanted it to last forever. I knew my workplace would be as flexible as they could, but I was considering not returning to work. Surprisingly, I found myself wanting to be a stay-at-home mum. As much as I had loved working and the buzz and energy it afforded me, I liked the possibility of being a domestic goddess. In truth this was another of my grand illusions, more daydreaming, and as much as I loved cooking, sewing, and gardening, I got bored fairly quickly.

And reality was always knocking at the door. Graeme's business was not bringing in enough money. The enormity of our financial future was silently stowed away in the *I can't think about that now* folder. It mattered hugely for Richard's future, but for now, in my ever-increasing denial, I just tucked it away.

I was totally in awe of the little creature we had created. I spent hours looking at Richard's limbs, smelling him, touching him, stroking him. I couldn't get enough. I still counted off his fingers and toes, reassuring myself he had all of them. With my finger, I would trace the outline of his mouth, his nose, his eyes. I patted down his hair; there was always a strand that stood upright, and it made him look like a cartoon character. When I bathed him, I stretched him out, one hand holding him from underneath, the other soaking the washer with warm water and squeezing the water all over his body. I would turn him onto his belly, holding up his chin, trying to get his little body used to water. All the while I'd be talking, telling him what I was doing, explaining each step. This was how it would be: if God was going to make him talk, I would help by talking all the time!

He was so incredibly beautiful to me; he had an aura of peace around him. At night I'd watch him sleep, his tiny chest rising and falling. He wasn't a particularly good sleeper, but it didn't matter. In a weird way I liked hearing him cry, because then I knew he was alive. When I watched him sleep, tears would often well up in my eyes, and my throat would tighten. My love for him was ever-present. At times I wondered where this Down syndrome thing was hiding. He was alert. His eyes always followed me and my voice. When he heard Graeme, his eyes would search for him. Even our dog would grab his attention, and he'd look around whenever Comet barked. He was connected; he knew his place in this world. He knew his home. There was little sign of how Down syndrome was affecting him.

When I breast-fed him, he'd put his hand up close to my nipple as if he wanted to make sure I knew he wanted this time with me, almost reassuring me that I was doing a good job. I became obsessed with breast-feeding; I had read that because babies with Down syndrome have protruding tongues and funny-shaped mouths, breast-feeding would help develop his control over his mouth. The sucking motion would improve the muscles in his mouth and ultimately improve his speech. Sometimes I would see his tongue pop out randomly. I'd gently place it back into his mouth with my finger.

Coming from a family of big talkers, and remembering how Pauline had often yelled rather than spoke, I knew this was the most important thing for me to focus on. He had to be able to talk. So whenever I had an opportunity to stick my boob in his mouth, I did, convinced that if he could communicate effectively with people, he would be able to get a job or let people know when he was lost and give them his phone number. Some people might consider it obsessive that I was fixated on his ability to speak when he was only two weeks old, but I was devoted to improving his chances in life. My other two requests to God could wait; this one started now.

Since Graeme worked from home, we were able to take on a lot of responsibilities together, yet we were each dealing with our son's disability in our own private way. Our grief was always disguised by our resolve—mine, to do everything I could to make Richard fit into the world by providing the best start we could through education, early intervention, and reading. Graeme took a different approach. To a certain extent his method was to ignore Down syndrome as much as he could and be ever-present in Richard's life: to ensure that he laughed when Rich cried, smiled at him when he was upset, watched TV with him, sang with him, and had fun with him. This was their way of being together and still is. Neither of us ever let our concern for his future or our sadness about what could have been—perhaps even our anger at the injustice of it all—dictate how we loved our son. Our love for him was all-encompassing. It withstood a tsunami of difficulties.

Our first appointment with the pediatrician loomed. I thought it both comical and almost sinister that Dr. Grass, the bearer of that heartbreaking news that had marred the most precious of days, was now a permanent member of our new village. Not only was she the newest member, but she was also the one who held our baby's life in her hands. I know that sounds hysterical—"held our baby's life in her hands"—but I really felt that, even though I knew he was pretty healthy.

I knew so little, and I wanted to know so much. How could I trust this woman? How could I even like her? But after our first appointment I liked her a great deal, and although Graeme and I always referred to her, childishly, as "Morticia," we knew she was an excellent medico. There was something in her calmness, in how she touched Richard, that gave me a lot of faith in her. She was not judging me or my son. She was, in fact, always reassuring me. As Richard grew older, she would no longer address me at the scheduled half-yearly appointments but spoke directly to him, crediting him with the intelligence to understand and take part in his own health. This set a benchmark that I would look for in others in the years to come.

There was concern about that hole in his heart, but it was slight. Even so, it was always in the back of my mind that there are specific medical conditions that only occur in children with Down syndrome. Was a catastrophe just around the corner? Was I going to catastrophize every aspect of his health from here on in? In hindsight, I realize this was the beginning of my anxiety. I had no control over how the dice would roll, and confronting that reality was wearing me down. All new parents have some sort of anxiety. It's natural. Having a kid with a disability just heightens those fears. Yet, as comical as mine might have appeared, there was always a risk factor that it had a root in something I read. However, at times it really was crazy. I once diagnosed Richard as having all the symptoms of leprosy. My doctor warned me that if I ever came into his room again with such nonsense, he would never see us again.

It was all starting to exhaust my emotional resources. My resolve to be "fine" was cracking, and so was I. There was always something that needed to be assessed, and we had monthly appointments at the baby clinic. I was always worried that Richard's measurements would fall below the average and I would be seen as a bad mother. Was his head big enough? Did he weigh enough? Did he pee enough? Did he drink enough? Were my boobs big enough? Did he have enough? Was I enough?

I watched the baby clinic nurse closely as she charted our monthly progress, ticking all the boxes that I was being a good mother. I was always a little teary attending these appointments, but I found our clinic midwife a breath of fresh air.

"Guess you must be finding all this very difficult, first baby and all, and also with Down syndrome," she said at our first appointment.

I so loved her forthrightness. Finally, here was someone with whom I didn't have to pretend I was buoyant. She was totally accepting of my situation.

"Well, yes. It's all a little overwhelming, and I am not sure if I am doing a good job."

Tears began streaming down my face. She was an old-fashioned country baby clinic nurse who had found herself unexpectedly in suburbia. Compassionate yet practical.

"Well, that's what I'm here for. Let's take off the little fellow's clothes and weigh him, and then we will measure him head to toe and a few other things."

Within half an hour she reassured me that Richard was healthy and growing along the right path and told me that I was an excellent mum and I wasn't to let anyone tell me otherwise. What she hadn't quite done, however, was convince me to believe that myself.

The most important appointment of my life was on the day we visited Macquarie University for the first time. If we didn't get into this program, anything else for Richard would be second best. Well, in reality, I meant that anything else would probably be second best for me. I'd had so many dreams and desires stomped on and killed off. I needed this win.

Although they had said yes, I still had this niggling concern they might change their minds. These were the people who had to help us nurture Richard to achieve his life's capacity. What I really wanted them to tell me was that he wasn't going to be dumb—that there was hope that he was not going to sit in a corner and dribble for the rest of his life. He was six weeks old. I was a nervous wreck.

Unfortunately, in the time since my phone call to Moira Pieterse, she had retired from her role at the program, leaving two staff members, Sue Cairns and Robin Treloar—both women in their mid-thirties who'd worked with Moira for several years—to look after the program. This put a new spin on everything. I was really annoyed that one of the world's leading experts on Down syndrome would not be looking after my son after all. Suddenly the way forward was going to be jeopardized by not having the great Moira Pieterse as part of our new village, but these much younger women instead. Of course, I had nothing to ground my disappointment. I just assumed that they couldn't be anywhere near as amazing as Moira. I was crazed with expectation, but I couldn't have been more wrong. Both highly qualified early intervention specialists, Sue and Robin could not have been more different. Sue was the pragmatic, extroverted one and Robin was quieter but equally determined to get the message across. In the coming years Sue and Robin would help us and our boy beyond measure.

More and more cracks splintered in my "perfect mum" façade as time wore on. But around me was a mountain of support. My baby clinic nurse was another of my rocks. Based in a little community center not far from home, her job was to ensure that new babies met their milestones, to check limbs, and basically to be the local monitor for the health of all new babies. I adored her enthusiasm and commitment to us both. Early on, she gave me details for my local new mothers' group, which would meet every month, mums and babies together. We all lived in the same area and therefore saw the same baby clinic nurse. As a group we were divided about what we thought of her. Some found her too abrupt, some too scary, while others adored her. She told it how she saw it and sometimes, when you are a bit fragile, that can be frightening.

They were a lovely group made up of hardworking, independent, upwardly mobile new mums who, like me, were all a little shell-shocked at having gone from their previous dynamic lives to one centered on breast-feeding, changing diapers, and severe sleep deprivation. They could see my struggles, and they, too, had their own new-mum issues. But none of them knew what it was like to care for an infant with Down syndrome. When Richard was the first of the babies to roll over onto his back, there was great surprise and concern that the disabled kid got there first. It was his finest hour so far. And mine, too. I drove home that day with a big smile on my face. I'd received the smallest of mercies.

On about my sixth visit to my baby clinic nurse, I completely broke down. I could not stop crying. I sobbed and sobbed. I was breaking. I had suffered my first panic attack the previous week and I was scared as hell that I was going crazy. I couldn't sleep, couldn't concentrate, and worst of all I couldn't eat. That never ever happens to me. I never lose my appetite—I could be on my deathbed and still have "a little something"—so I knew my mental state was in a bad way. I could pretend most days, to Graeme, family, and friends, that I was fine. I couldn't let them know I was not coping. I am always "Just fine, thanks."

The clinic nurse wiped away the tears. She listened to me and gave me the details of a postnatal depression group I could attend. It had recently become better understood that many mums, regardless of their baby's health, suffered postnatal depression, and as a government initiative funding was allocated to help facilitate groups of mums to alleviate the more advanced "baby blues." The group sounded like salvation, a place where I could talk about not coping along with other not-coping mums and avoid judgment. I enrolled straightaway.

Thankfully, I also had my local Down syndrome mothers' group, which met every couple of months. Some of these women would become my lifelong friends. In those early days we gave each other a great deal of support, comfort, and knowledge. I felt the most at ease in this mothers' group. They could empathize with my tears and fears. They could see the distress and uncertainty written all over my face. Some of these mums had spent more time than me in Down Syndrome Land and had more of a handle on it. I found these women and their families a calming influence on my life. We'd meet at someone's house or in a park. We would take lovely food to eat and chitchat about our concerns. At times I'd cry, and others would reassure me it would get easier. What remains vivid from that time is my feeling of protection and security when I was with this group. They helped ease the difficulties of the unknown. They were also in the unknown, on this wild trip they had not expected. We'd mark the milestones in our children's lives just like any mothers. We would celebrate the smallest achievements, like a first tooth or a poop in the toilet.

Despite such encouragement and enthusiasm, I found I still needed more and more support. I could hardly get enough. Not long after Richard was born, I had called my local Down syndrome office for some help. I spoke with an amazing woman, Carolyn. Over time she got to know it was me on the phone, since I must have called her just about every day with a new ridiculous question. "He hasn't pooped in two days. Is that normal?" "He wouldn't take the breast this morning. Is that normal?" "He slept an extra hour. Is that normal?" She was patient. She was also the mother of eighteen-year-old Bradley.

"Can I ask you what Bradley is like?"

"Well, he is Bradley. He is just that: our son Bradley."

From that day on that became my mantra.

"He's just Richard."

And he was just Richard. He was just Richard when he cried. He was just Richard when he smiled. And he was just Richard when one morning when he was about eight months old, he looked at me, and held up his arms. He spoke only one word, a word that brought tears to my eyes.

"Mum," he said.

# 3

# Slings and Arrows

"Life is all about evolution. What looks like a mistake to others has been a milestone in my life. Even if people have betrayed me, even if my heart was broken, even if people misunderstood or judged me, I have learned from these incidents. We are human and we make mistakes, but learning from them is what makes the difference."

—AMISHA PATEL

"They're just so special, aren't they?"

"Nice to see them out and about."

"My niece has one of those."

Down syndrome is one of the most recognizable disabilities. There is no doubting these children are different, because their physical features say so, but there seems to be an unspoken rule that says people are allowed to comment on that difference. In your presence. Using loud voices. In the supermarket. At the bus stop. There have been many times I could have commented on what people said. "Special? No, not really. They have tantrums and tummy aches, meltdowns and magical moments, toys and toilet training, like any other kid." "Out and about? They're not serial killers. We don't cage them. They can come and go as they please." "She has one of *those*? What model and year? It is high-maintenance?"

People forget that *one of those* is someone's daughter or son, or sister or brother, and he or she has feelings. I have concluded that there are people who seriously believe that if you are disabled you don't have feelings, that you don't get hurt by inappropriate behavior or stares. People with Down syndrome have the same range of emotions as everyone else. The difference is they are sometimes not allowed to show them, or they lack the vocabulary to express them, and sometimes their caregivers are not patient enough to allow them the time they might need to come to terms with them.

"Mum, why is that person staring at me?" Richard has asked me many times.

Depending on my mood, the response could be "Because you are so beautiful" or "Because they're bloody rude."

I'm not perfect, but I can attest to the fact that I've never been in a supermarket or at a bus stop and leaned over and said to Richard, "My goodness, why doesn't that mother get her daughter's ears fixed?" or "If I was his mother, I'd be doing something about that acne" or "What a slack mum, letting her child get so fat." I wouldn't dream of saying such things, so why do others think it's all right to comment about people who have a disability, especially within earshot?

Not all people are so rude, of course. But even strangers who express sympathy don't realize what an intrusion it actually is. At times I'm okay with it, because it means, at the very least, connection, and if connection leads to acceptance, then that's progress, exhausting as it is. When you have a child with a disability, you are co-opted into becoming an advocate whether you want to be or not.

The ones I find most offensive are those "good" people who want to tell you how truly "blessed" you are and how you should consider yourself "lucky." Once, in a supermarket, a perfect stranger approached me with this precise sentiment. I looked over to see Richard drooling, his eyes crossed over and snot everywhere. *Yes, lucky me,* I thought as I did my best not to kill this stranger on the spot.

I understand that occasionally some things are said out of embarrassment by people who feel awkward in these situations. They will say the first thing that pops into their heads to overcome their discomfort. I know what they're thinking: *This woman has a child that is not normal.* There have been many times throughout Richard's life when well-meaning platitudes have embarrassed me, irked me, or just made me laugh out loud. I am not the only mum of a child with Down syndrome who has had that experience. Some of us laugh about it, some of us put up a good fight, and others, well, they agree. To each their own. Whatever helps us cope.

It did make me feel better on occasion. Meaningless words often gave me hope, some light, and commonality with many of the other parents in the same boat. It was a camaraderie of sorts, telling ourselves what a lucky bunch we were. I am sure that at the beginning we all needed to hold on to something that could give our lives a sense of normality. However, it never lasted long. Soon enough, the difficulty of the situation left me questioning God's goodness. His "blessings"? Really? "You are blessed" became a particular favorite of mine for a while. I wanted to truly believe that I was blessed, but the more reality sank in, the more I felt my life was very *unblessed*. How could this be my life? This was not what was meant to happen. *Please God,* I thought, *unbless me and give your blessing to someone else more capable.* I so wanted to tell well-wishers, "Here, if you feel I am so blessed, you take this on. You take over."

"Oh, you will just love Maryanne. She has a son with Down syndrome, too."

Really?

Just because I have a son with Down syndrome and Maryanne has a son with Down syndrome, it's assumed that we will instantly bond, be Facebook friends, meet for endless coffee dates, and perhaps tour Europe together. Added to that, the respective sons will like each other straightaway, have loads in common, and demand sleepovers within an hour of meeting. It doesn't matter if Maryanne is a right-wing voter, doesn't like animals, and watches *Baywatch*. Never mind whether we have anything else in common; we both have sons with

Down syndrome, so it's a given that we will instantly click. No. Both having sons with Down syndrome does not a friendship make. The friendships that I made in my Down syndrome group initially began because of our kids, who all had Down syndrome, yet it was the other commonalities that forged our friendships: our sense of humor, our passions, our interests.

"Oh, they are such loving children" is the other one that makes me cringe. Is it that extra chromosome that endows them with the love gene, maybe? I don't think so. I can honestly say after many years of knowing a wide range of children with Down syndrome that some of them can be just as rude and irritating as the rest of us. And it doesn't change when they become adults, either. I can guarantee you that.

Richard was a loving child, but so am I a loving person. So's his dad, and he has a wider family that shares a lot of love. We are all affectionate and kind, so our kids are too. As a toddler, if Richard liked someone, he would hug them. It was kind of cool, really, that hugging came so easily to him. It was like a gift he was always ready to give. But if Richard doesn't like you, he'll let you know it. He has a good bullshit detector when it comes to reading people's responses to him. As a child, he could sense others' discomfort; he could tell when he was being judged, stared at, or talked about.

On one occasion when Rich was three, we had a visitor, a close work colleague, who was clearly uncomfortable with his attempts at engaging with her. The more he stumbled over his words, the more she ignored him, whereupon he calmly went and collected her handbag and handed it to her, making no bones about the fact she should leave. Her jaw dropped. She left, and we never heard from her again. She was not the only friend we lost who couldn't handle being around our "blessed" child.

"They all just love music." Oh, save me! So does the rest of the world. Who could not like music? Like the rest of us, music gives people with Down syndrome great joy, at times comfort, and an opportunity to communicate even if they lack the ability to do so verbally. If you went to any preschool anywhere from Massachusetts to Moscow to Mauritius, every single young kid would most likely dance if you played music. The fact that kids with Down syndrome like music is because humans—and even a lot of animals—like music, too.

In hindsight, I could have been better at guiding those who uttered such commonplace sentiments away from these hurtful generalizations. Perhaps they meant well, but bundling all people with Down syndrome into the same basket is wrong. It elides their real possibilities and their real individuality. It failed to recognize the joy that I have being Richard's mum. Not a kid with Down syndrome, but my flesh and blood.

⋊

It was not only strangers who offered what they thought was good advice or sympathy, or both. And it was not always directed at Richard. Soon after Richard was born and we brought him home, I received another visit from the social worker who had come to see me in the hospital.

I was put off from the start when she shooed Comet away. She didn't like dogs. Although Comet was a good-natured kelpie-corgi mix and would lick you to death, the social worker just didn't want him anywhere near her. She was a neurotic, edgy sort of woman, and poor Comet had to relinquish his comfortable spot on the sofa for the cool outside for the rest of her visit. If he could have taken a bite out of her, I think he would have.

"What is that rash around his neck?" she asked, pointing to Richard lying in his crib.

I told her he drooled a lot. I thought she might have known that babies with Down syndrome drool a lot; actually a lot of new babies drool a lot. Surely, if you are visiting a home with a Down syndrome child, you should be familiar with the features and problems? It was her job to know these things.

"How are you coping? It's quite normal to feel frustrated and even angry or even take it out on the child."

Was she suggesting I had hurt my baby?

I told her again that the rash was because of drooling. I could feel my anger rising, but I knew I had to keep my cool. If I lost my temper now, she might deem me a person with anger management issues and have my child removed, thinking that I was an unstable mother with a disabled child at risk. She looked at me with the pitying expression I had already become accustomed to. She lowered her voice before she spoke.

"Are you coping with this?"

I took a deep breath and told her I was coping, that the rash was being attended to, and we had a lot of family and other support. I couldn't wait for her to leave. I never saw her again, but her visit left me with a bitter taste in my mouth. It wasn't just my son on display. I, too, was being observed, poked, and prodded. I, too, was being judged.

❧

In those early years, I could never really fully engage in other people's lives. I kept most of my old and new friends at a distance. I even felt a distance with my family. Something was different with me. My light had faded. Perhaps I didn't want them looking too deeply into my heart. I was always on the outside looking in, fearful and cautious. A hypervigilance pervaded my interactions with people, especially with those I didn't know.

"Hello, I'm Benny, and my son, Richard, has Down syndrome."

That is how I'd introduce myself. I did it because I didn't want to be caught off guard. I didn't want to see that all-too-familiar "pity" face. New conversations are about information: "Where do you work?" "Where do you live?" "Have you got kids?" It's that last question that would undo me. Instead of being proud of my son and championing his achievements, I crumbled inside and felt teary. I didn't want that to be the sum of my love for Richard. Tears instead of joy would set the "pity" face, but if I offered that information first, then I couldn't be pitied. I would catch *them* off guard and lead by example.

For all the hurt and frustration that the outside world can bring, even those within the Down syndrome community aren't always warm and fuzzy. Like any other group, it has its agitators, its oh-so-politically-correct group, and those who take on the cause with such zealotry that you feel totally inadequate in their presence. Members of this community can be very judgmental and cause other parents to feel that the choices they make will somehow diminish their child's capacity to thrive. In my experience, being judged can lead to feelings of inadequacy and worthlessness and often to mental health issues such as anxiety and depression. I allowed this to happen to me. It is complicated enough when we judge ourselves, as some of us regularly do, but to be judged by our peers and contemporaries is unconscionable. What's best for you may not be right for others. Your lived experience is just your own. Plain and simple.

In any community there is competition, and the Down syndrome community is no different. I am sure there have been plenty of mums like me who would have liked their offspring to be the brightest and best Down syndrome person on the planet. As a young fellow at Macquarie University, Richard was just awesome: he was a bright light about the place and connected so well with all the staff and other parents. You'd think he could become prime minister, he was doing so well.

Although there was huge support for his success, other parents still wanted their own child to succeed more or to have greater happiness. That is only natural. There is a desperation for services, for sourcing the most capable occupational therapist, for finding the mainstream school that will take children with intellectual disabilities or the dentist who loves children with Down syndrome. It is a never-ending battle, not only against the system, but also with your peers, who seem to have already mastered the jargon and the therapies and the homework. There is real envy of the kid who is most liked or more successful.

I remember feeling so full of myself when I announced to my Down syndrome mothers' group that the director of the local pre-school was making an exception for Richard. Although he was not yet three, she insisted she "just had to have him" at her preschool. I also gloated on the occasion I announced Richard was going to the day care center at my work, which had a total inclusion policy, where children like Richard work alongside other children at the preschool.

That was nothing, however, compared to my condescending announcement that we had no trouble getting him into Mount Kuring-gai Primary School at age five (when in fact I, like others, had been disappointed many times over by other schools not wanting to take him). I was behaving with little understanding of the pain that some families had experienced while attempting to find a place for their child at a local primary school. My problem was, of course, that it was all about *my* son. *Woo-hoo, we got in! Woo-hoo, my son is smart and I'm a good mum!* In my twenty-eight-plus years in this community, I have seen plenty of other mums behave like this, and I have even been upset by their actions. (Hypocrisy, anyone?) It just goes to show that all of us are capable of inconsiderate behavior, even those of us with the best of intentions.

The not-for-profit disability sector is teeming with people—great people—who've got loads of good intentions, but I have learned over the years that many of them come with their own agenda and baggage, including the bureaucrats in the field. Out among the larger disability community, there have been times I've found it both challenging and dumbfounding. Decisions can be made purely from ego rather than for the greater good. Once, a perfectly good, functioning disability service was closed down (or "remodeled") because the new CEO needed to make his or her mark. It's a funny thing that, although you are a parent and live and breathe a disability, an "expert" in the field will often fob you off as "emotional" because you can't provide empirical evidence. Really, now!

I have friends who have kids with other intellectual disabilities who find kids with Down syndrome a real thorn in their side. It's not that they don't like our kids; it's just that there seems to be more sympathy in the wider world for our group. People judge the parent if at playgroup your child acts aggressively and they can see no obvious reason why, no telltale physical characteristics that might label the child as "disabled." All they see is unreasonable behavior and no sense of calm or connection. But underneath are many possibilities: kids with autism, fragile X syndrome, or some form of developmental delay. All these kids may act unconventionally and not receive the same understanding a child with a visible disability gets.

As challenging as that is, I must admit that at times I sometimes feel jealous of the parents of those kids. A child who is autistic still looks like his mum and dad. Although I see parts of me in Richard, I would have liked a child who looked more like me. I know that sounds weird, but it was part of the dream. But he looks like a person with Down syndrome, with a hint of me and a hint of Graeme. Like a drop of color in a two-liter can of white paint.

When a close friend of mine got pregnant at the age of forty-eight, it was, to say the least, a great surprise. And, yes, there was cause for concern for her and the baby's health. I happened to run into her father and without a second thought congratulated him on his upcoming grandfather role.

"Well, I am not sure about it all. She has to have all those tests. We don't want any mongoloids in the family."

Mongoloid? When was the last time anyone actually used that term? Stunned, I quickly gathered my thoughts, holding back the tears, and made my excuses to remove myself from his presence. I wanted to say so much but said nothing. This man clearly knew that Richard had Down syndrome. Didn't he realize what he'd said? Probably not.

When Richard was little, I was fearful. I didn't want to alienate anyone. I needed support even from those who said such offensive things. Words like "retard," "spaz," and "mongoloid" are so damaging. In the past I stayed silent. I screamed inside *Please don't say that!* but never had the courage to say anything aloud. Now I have the courage to correct people. I say, "Do you think that word is appropriate?" or "I find that word really offensive." Or if I am feeling particularly pissed off: "You are kidding me, aren't you? Do you know how offensive that is?" I no longer fear retribution or alienation. I simply don't care what people think anymore. All I care about is that people with disabilities receive the respect and acknowledgment they deserve.

~

I must be cautious when I reflect. In truth, I was not such a great kid, amusing myself with mimicking Pauline and other kids with disabilities, making my sisters and friends laugh at their expense. The cruel, silly world of children. It is with that reflection, though, that I can see the power of inclusion for people with an intellectual disability into the mainstream school system. Most people of my generation never had the opportunity to have a close relationship with anyone with an intellectual disability. Certainly not at school and very rarely in our immediate world.

In Australia until the late 1970s, it was routine for many new parents of a baby with Down syndrome to be, in the words of Carolyn Smith, "handed a prepared set of papers authorizing the admittance of the baby to a private institution for permanent care" and told to "go home, forget you had this child, and start again." Pieterse's research through the Macquarie program in effect challenged not just the bleak diagnosis that accompanied the birth of a child with Down syndrome but the very notion of medically defined intelligence and how varying abilities can be accommodated within society. As Pieterse explains, "My idea of what intelligence is about is the interaction between genetic potential and appropriate environmental stimulation at any particular time. But that was within a culture of the medical profession saying to these mothers, '*Don't worry about this one, it won't amount to anything, it'll probably die early, it probably won't learn to walk until seven or eight or something, probably won't ever talk, it'll drag your whole family down, it'll wreck your marriage.*'" You name it, there's this litany. "*Go home and have another one, forget it, get rid of it.*" And, in fact, in those days quite a lot of parents did.

Many of the institutions, where up to an estimated 80 percent of babies with Down syndrome were sent, were privately owned and operated by doctors. Moira recalled, "There was one in particular [run] by a nurse called Matron Eaton. Matron Eaton's at Wentworth Falls was very well known and recommended by all the pediatricians as where they would send their baby . . . [I]t would be very well kept. And it was run to spotless nursing methods with absolute sensory deprivation and it was just extraordinary! Everything spotlessly clean with the bottle pumped into one side and [the children] propped up against something. But no loving or touching or cuddling or anything that's so essential to baby development."

According to data from the state of Victoria, in 1969 the life expectancy of a child with Down syndrome in Australia was ten years of age, so schooling options were not a pressing priority. Most children would have died from lack of medical treatment for routinely treated illnesses and diseases such as pneumonia and cardiac conditions. Where a non–Down syndrome child would receive corrective treatment and medications, children with Down syndrome were only considered for "palliative" medical options.

When I was growing up, there were only special schools—out of sight, out of mind. I do recall that we had one girl in our class who perhaps, looking back, may have been on the autism spectrum, but there was little in the way of diagnosis at that time. Often kids on any spectrum were seen as simply stupid, with behavioral problems.

In 1992 the passage of the Disability Discrimination Act (DDA) by the Australian parliament made it illegal to treat people unfairly because of a disability. Still active today, the DDA promotes equal rights, equal opportunity, and equal access for people with disabilities. Inclusive education has been legally supported in Australia since 1992 and recommended by the United Nations since 1994.

From 1991 states and territories around Australia passed their versions of Disability Service Acts. The act made it clear that people with disability have the same human rights as other people in the community. This includes the same rights to education and health care. There had been many machinations of the legislation but in 2013 the Australian federal government introduced the National Disability Insurance Scheme. The national roll-out of funding began in July 2016. The NDIS is a person-centered approach to enabling people with disability to participate in all aspects of society. It is based on an insurance model in which the consumer chooses how they want to spend their allocated funds and, most importantly, chooses the service provider. The scheme is planned to be fully operational across Australia by 2019.

Both the commonwealth and state acts opened the way for people to have legal recourse. Public institutions such as schools could no longer refuse enrollment of a student on the grounds that they had a disability. In 2008 the commonwealth government ratified the United Nations Declaration on the Rights of Disabled Persons, further supporting the idea of inclusion as a human right.

Today, all Australian schools have obligations towards students with disability under the Disability Discrimination Act 1992 (the DDA) and the Disability Standards for Education 2005 (the Standards). The Standards require that all Australian schools ensure students with disabilities are able to access and participate in education on the same basis as students without disability.

The bulk of the research shows that inclusion in mainstream school produces better academic outcomes for children with disabilities. A 2008 review of international research on inclusion versus segregation found that no review in *forty years* had come out in favor of educational segregation. The bottom line? "Inclusion leads not only to better education but acceptance, interaction, and friendship."

Dr. Thomas Hehir of the Harvard Graduate School of Education documented the results of a systematic review of 280 studies from 25 countries and found "clear and consistent evidence that inclusive educational settings can confer substantial short- and long-term benefits for students with *and* without disabilities." The report also found that "research has demonstrated that, for the most part, including students with disabilities in regular education classes does not harm non-disabled students and may even confer some academic and social benefits . . . Several recent reviews have found that, in most cases, the impacts on non-disabled students of being educated in an inclusive classroom are either neutral or positive."

Yet, interestingly, when you look at abuse and bullying in school, alarm bells ring. According to the results of the Children and Young People with Disability Australia (CYDA) 2016 national survey of bullying of students with disability:

- 67 percent of respondents stated that students with disability do not receive adequate support at school.
- Over half (52 percent) of students with disability have been bullied. This is significantly higher than the 27 percent of the total student population who report bullying.
- 34 percent of students with disability have been excluded from a range of curricular and extracurricular activities at school. This includes activities such as camps, dances, and formals.
- Nearly one in five (19 percent) students with disability have experienced restraint at school, including physical, mechanical, chemical and psychosocial restraints.
- 19 percent of students with disability have experienced seclusion at school.
- 12 percent of students with disability attend school part-time.

- 8 percent of students with disability have been refused enrollment.

Although we've come a long way, I think the more we recognize the power of reaching out and the power that language has to help or harm each other, the more success we will have at building a world that embraces and encourages everyone, with or without disabilities.

The great social upheaval across the Western world in the late 1960s and early 1970s was characterized by various rights movements (also called "identity politics" because of its emphasis on individual rights): civil rights, women's rights, and also disability rights. The disability rights movement saw a shift from the "medical model" of disability (that the disability resided in the person and was a health issue to be fixed or managed by medical treatments) to the "social model' (which proposed that disability was socially constructed and it wasn't necessarily the person who needed to be "fixed" but the physical and social environment they operated within).

In 1971 the United Nations General Assembly proclaimed the Declaration on the Rights of Mentally Retarded Persons. In 1975 the Declaration on the Rights of Disabled Persons outlined a number of social, economic, civil, and political rights for people with disabilities.

The recognition of the rights of people with disabilities was taken up in Australia and reflected in the various state and federal legislations as well as various rights groups and advocacy organizations that were established by people with disabilities such as People with Disability Australia, the Council for Intellectual Disability, and the Physical Disability Council. The legal progress has also helped shift the conversation, educate people, and hopefully has cut down the number of thoughtless comments—although obviously there's still a lot of room for improvement.

❧

I still find the shitty things people say and do unnerving at times. That also goes for the politics of disability, too, which can be so complicated. I am sure others also find it that way. For many years I chose not to live in that world, because I really didn't like it. It scared me and saddened me. But eventually I learned to accept that although it can be scary and sad, it is also funny, rewarding, difficult, lovely, and certainly never dull.

If you are reading this, about to have a little person with Down syndrome, or already have one, here is a little list of dos and don'ts that might help:

- Don't look into the future. Just be present in the here and now. One day at a time.
- Don't feel you have to put on your happy face. If you're cranky or anxious or depressed—or all three—then tell someone and get some help. You are human and not super-mum or -dad.
- Don't beat yourself up. Shit happens to the best of us. Be kind to yourself.
- Don't forget that your baby is just like any other baby. Like any infant, a baby with Down syndrome needs what any other baby needs: nourishment, sleep, clean diapers, hugs, love, and kisses.
- Do keep yourself nice. As my mum says: "A little bit of lippy goes a long way" even when you don't feel like it.
- Do eat well, get some exercise, and take time out for you.
- Don't feel you have to take on anyone else's opinions or thoughts. Your baby is your baby and you will know him or her better than anyone else.
- Do refrain from slapping people when they are condescending or they make some thoughtless, insensitive comment. You can, however, tell them to fuck off!
- Do read up! There is a lot of good information out there on Down syndrome. And join your local DS association.
- Do laugh! Sometimes life is just funny, and that's okay.

# 4

# Primary Colors

"It is time for parents to teach young people early on
that in diversity there is beauty and there is strength."
—MAYA ANGELOU

"My grandson goes to Macquarie University."

Richard's nan, Cecily, didn't bother to enlighten her acquaintances as to what he was doing there. She was just delighted that her grandson was attending a university. She refused to see Richard as anything but her beautiful grandson, who was just like anybody else.

"He's got a little bit of Downs," she told her friends.

We had all come to the university from various surrounding suburbs. Most of the families came from largely affluent areas. I felt a sense of guilt, or perhaps my working-class roots got to me, because early intervention in those days was not common and so little was available. However, I'd throw away my guilt at the drop of a hat: when it came to Richard being accepted into Macquarie, I would have thrown my mother under a bus.

In this new village, the twenty families who attended the program tried hard to encourage each other. Every week Graeme, Richard, and I would attend one-on-one sessions that taught us various techniques and strategies for getting Richard prepared for preschool, primary school, and, well, basically life. Graeme was considered a bit of a rock star, since he was one of the few dads who attended. The two of us had to commit to implementing at home what we learned at Macquarie. The pressure was on, and I was relentless. If I couldn't go to a university session because I was at work, I would grill Graeme afterward to ensure he'd covered all bases. He was much more laid-back than I was, and this started to concern me. We were like the hare and the tortoise. All I could think about was that we had to get Richard ready for primary school.

We were taught about gross motor and fine motor skills and how to incorporate them into everyday life. When we were just sitting, watching television, I would have him facing me and hold his arms, his little legs on my thighs, and I would get him to go up and down so his legs would get stronger. Every play game became an exercise for Richard. We learned about the importance of speech therapy and how to maintain eye contact and keep our child's concentration. It was overwhelming, that combination of so much jargon and the pressure of my own making. If this child was ever going to reach his full potential, we were to become drill sergeants. Everything we learned would ultimately have an effect in Richard's adult years. Stacking measuring cups would eventually help him with math; getting him to crawl with his legs pretty much taped together would help with balance; blowing bubbles would help with making his words sound right. And on and on it went. Welcome to Disability World. I didn't want to be in this world. It scared me. I didn't belong here. I wanted to be in "normal" world. I so desperately wanted to leave but couldn't.

Each session I would take notes and ask questions, wanting Robin and Sue to secretly tell me Richard was by far the best student they had. I worked hard to hide my desire to hold up white A4 cards with scores on them in big black numbers, like a judging panel at the Olympics: "Richard, your scores today were 8, 8.5, 9. My goodness, the judge at the end gave you a 10!"

The one-on-one sessions lasted about a year, and Richard responded very well. He was a joyful child; his cheeky grin and giggle endeared him to so many people around him. He was captivating.

Once you had the Richard bug, you became a fan. It helped me relax a little. I was no longer Bernadette; I was Richard's mum. That was cool, and I was so proud of him—and of us.

>

At eighteen months, Richard was crawling, hitting milestones. He was making progress—yay!—but my mental health was challenged with ongoing anxiety. I could not shake it off. There was a heaviness on my chest and shoulders that would not leave me. I slept poorly. Tears were always only a nanosecond away. *Please don't ask me how I am; I will fall apart before your eyes.* There was dread and an overwhelming sense of failure and fear. I kept the smiling "I'm fine" face, but I wasn't fine—and yet life was there to be lived. Richard needed me. I had to hold it together as best I could.

Around this time, my father-in-law, Phil, died tragically and far too quickly. The disease took rapid hold of his body and quickly overwhelmed it. Our grief was extreme; Graeme was left inconsolable. Gone was his hero, his confidant. What was left was a family hurting from this enormous loss, a mother-in-law who for so long knew only life with her husband, and now a grandchild with an intellectual disability. Life appeared to hold little meaning. We had to focus on something positive, something tangible.

I returned to work at the Australian Broadcasting Corporation (ABC). I was back with the team at Enterprises, in the retail and distribution arm. Part of me wanted to stay at home, be a mum, be cheerful Carol Brady. It was about the same time that Richard made it clear he didn't want to be breast-fed anymore. I was shattered but had to accept this new stage. He started drinking from a cup, so the need to be with him 24-7 was no longer there.

Work was always good for me. I loved being surrounded by people who were creative, clever, and generally left leaning, which I felt would be safer for a mum with a child with Down syndrome. A more accepting place, one of tolerance. For the most part, that was the case.

My own division was full of people who wrapped me up in the safety of familiarity. I felt relieved, like I was going home.

At first I was apprehensive about approaching the day care center's director. I was never quite sure how people would look upon Down syndrome, so I had my stomach in my throat. But Helen, the director of the ABC crèche, says it was never an issue for them having a child with a disability. Graeme could now concentrate on his work, and he was now taking Richard to Macquarie for the group sessions on his own.

Work gave me a purpose, a reason to get on with something like a normal life. I was already sick of the world of disability. It was starting to define my family and me and I didn't want that. I actively hated it. I loved being in a dynamic workplace where I could hold Disability World at arm's length. I was really good at what I did. I knew that, and it made me feel stronger about what lay ahead. It was my armor, but if you pierced it, blood would run. Gazing through my rose-tinted glasses, I had assumed that having Richard at the crèche with other children from like-minded parents would leave me free of scrutiny or judgment. After all, this was a workplace that nurtured diversity and difference.

But a reality slap is never far away, and judgment can be thinly disguised as concern. One day, after asking me some highly personal questions, a fellow crèche parent asked why I hadn't taken action to have a termination before Richard was born. Inside I was absolutely gutted, but I tried to deal with the question as best I could. Tears started to well up, along with that feeling of being less than—not good enough for—this woman. So I told her I hadn't had any testing, but what I should have said was "How dare you ask me that? Mind your own freakin' business." But of course I didn't. I wanted to be accepted—and more importantly, I wanted Richard to be. To Helen's great credit, she later called that parent in to let her know she'd acted in a thoughtless, discriminatory, and unkind way. As Helen has since said of the incident, "Richard was loved, valued, and he made a great contribution to the center. We all benefited from having him and his family as part of our community there, and I wanted people to know that acceptance and embracing diversity was what we wanted and advocated for."

How lucky I was to have such an advocate for Richard! People like Helen make all the difference in this world. They have your back, they make change happen, and they are not scared of reprimanding people for saying something inappropriate. What was evident to me at the time was that I should assume nothing and have no expectations—and that I should hold my own counsel. My anger was never far from the surface, but neither was my optimism. Little gestures of help, conversation, and genuine concern meant the day could be much better.

Receiving so much stimulation at the crèche was brilliant for Richard. He had loads of kids to play with and learn from. I had to learn also that, regardless of Richard having Down syndrome, he was still a kid and one, apparently, with a temper as healthy as mine. The day he bit the little boy who stole his toy sent me into a total panic. All hell broke loose as parents had to be called and apologies made. In fact, I was just a little proud of Richard for having the wherewithal to defend his toy. And why shouldn't he? I had not yet taught him how to say "Fuck off," so biting had to do for now.

At about two and a half, Richard was now trying to walk but having problems with balance. When he wasn't at the ABC day care center, he was now joining in group sessions at Macquarie two days a week, just small classes covering the next phase of the learning process. This was getting the little ones ready for preschool: preparing them to be attentive, sit still, and play games. It was funny seeing seven or eight little faces that all have that similar "veil," yet each with the slightest of family resemblance clearly marking their tribe. They were changing, these kids. They were no longer babies. Each had his or her own little personality: some bossy, some quiet, some naughty—just like other children. However, these children had a lot of work to do. They were placed in a classroom with a windowed wall. We could see them, but they couldn't see us. We had to observe what the teacher was doing, and we were to do the same at home.

As in any situation, you like some folks a lot more than others, and I certainly made some truly valuable friends and confidantes. There were also mums and dads who you just plain didn't connect with regardless of the fact that our kids had the same genetic curiosity. My two besties, Sally and Karen, held values similar to mine. We would laugh, cry, and console, but most of all we understood the spoken support that we gave each other. We knew that all these little children were ours, and we cherished them. Spending time outside of Macquarie was also important, and we would often meet up for coffee and of course spend endless hours on the phone.

We all saw the importance of dressing our kids well. If they were going to look different, we were all determined to dress them better than other kids. There was no shortage: OshKosh, Nike, designer wear, and the best footwear. Our kids sported the latest haircuts and spectacles. At one stage I worked out that Richard had a better wardrobe than I did.

We all wanted our kids to grow, learn, and thrive, to be finally ready for that all-important first day at a regular primary school. Despite my dread, I eventually became accustomed to Disability World. I could see that Richard was responding well. He was engaging with others, he was doing stuff, and he was succeeding at it. At times it was if his little lightbulb went on. There were some things he was just plain crap at, and we had to work hard to get him to reach his milestones; but when he got one, we would jump for joy. Having remembered my promise to God, speech was the most important. Graeme and I never stopped talking to Richard. We also sang, made up rhymes, and commented on everything we saw. It did the trick, as these days I have to tell Richard "Please shut up and stop talking!" Be careful what you wish for.

But just when I thought everything was going along merrily and I was totally in step with the program and my anxieties calmed, some bastard self-promoting professor turned our world upside down with the news the center would close in six months, to be replaced with a research program instead. We had been there only three years. I felt sick.

The safety net was being taken away.

Over the years I have observed a great deal about the academic world. Most professors, researchers, and tutors do excellent work that helps us all to live fuller, richer lives. Certainly the program we attended at Macquarie led to a better understanding of how children with Down syndrome can learn, participate, and be fully included in regular classes. It also taught students learning to be special needs teachers to better understand how to bring out the best in these kids.

The center's extensive program paved the way for educators not just to accept children with Down syndrome into their classrooms but to embrace them as well. This is still an ongoing struggle but no longer a battle. Kids with Down syndrome are sometimes put into mainstream classes and sometimes into what is called specialist support classes, which is not always ideal if the family wants total inclusion.

Had the center remained open, the possibilities could have been endless. I believe this move was so shortsighted, but apparently research dollars are easier to come by. It looks more impressive on a résumé running a research program than an early intervention program. I'm not sure why they could not have run both. To me it was the essence of discrimination. We thought of many ways to keep the center or something similar operating. Early intervention programs were sparse. Certain places specialized in physical therapy, and you could see someone else about speech therapy, but there was very little to help our kids get ready for preschool, let alone primary school. When Richard was born, I was asked by a mother of a friend of mine if I was going to keep him. "You know there are places you can send him," she said, meaning an institution.

Richard's future was now hanging in the balance as far as I was concerned. Where would we go from here? What would we do? Panic. Some of the parents joined forces to create an early intervention program outside the university. Lifestart was a vision of my friend Sally.

In part she was successful, but it took a good year to source the funds she needed, source a venue, employ staff, etc. That early intervention program continues to this day. Graeme and I thought it best to look elsewhere, as I didn't feel we could wait for the new program to get started. We discovered a newly opened program that had just started at a special school a short distance from where we lived. It was not designed just for kids with Down syndrome but for a myriad of intellectual disabilities. We applied and were accepted. The teacher was a gorgeous young woman full of enthusiasm. She was positive and caring. As delighted as I was to have found this program, I was nervous about being at a school that didn't just specialize in Down syndrome but covered the full spectrum of intellectual disabilities.

I had just started getting comfortable in the world of Down syndrome, but this new, bigger world was totally alien to me. It really frightened me. Being confronted by a six-foot-tall young man built like a sumo wrestler but with the cognition of a five-year-old is disarming. Screams and unruliness accompanied the walk from car park to classroom on Richard's first day there. With each step I held him closer, tighter. I was scared and completely uncomfortable. *Why can't these kids be controlled?* I wondered. These were shameful thoughts. My own discrimination was coming into play as I wondered whether we'd made the right decision.

At about the same time, I was recruited by a large international book club. It was an opportunity that was extremely tempting. The financial offer would have been an enormous help to my family. The job had excellent prospects, but I was also torn with leaving the ABC, a job I truly loved, plus there was still the child care center, which was so convenient. Graeme and I had to think long and hard about what to do. Amazingly, as all this was going on, I happened to meet with the director of a local preschool. Although Richard was not yet three, she was happy to make an exception to take him in the following term. I jumped at an opportunity, as I didn't have to fight for inclusion. They wanted Richard. They offered a one-on-one teacher's aide to help with some of Richard's challenges, which mostly revolved around the fine motor skills. An inclusive Kindergarten Union preschool. *Thank you, God.* It was now 1994, and a new phase in Richard's life was about to begin. At times I had to pinch myself with how fortunate we had been. God was looking after me after all.

I accepted the book club job, and Richard was now enrolled two days a week at Wahroonga Pre-School, a mainstream preschool with only one other child who had special needs. The parents and children at the preschool were kind and accepting. There was only one woman who asked whether Down syndrome was "contagious." I remember that episode clearly. I can still see her face. Hardly able to believe my ears, I remember that I laughed and walked away. What else could I do?

The new job meant that I now had a great deal of responsibility, with a hefty workload, long hours, a very flashy company car, and international travel. It all sounded very glamorous, and in a way it was; but like anything that sounds that good, it came at a price. And that price was less time at home, less time with Richard and Graeme, and less time for myself. I soon become a workaholic and the cracks began to widen. The pressure of sustaining that lifestyle was causing me concern, but I retreated to my usual tactic of hiding it away somewhere, to be dealt with at another time. Richard was settled into preschool. Their job was to get him prepared for primary school. And they did.

Richard, now four, was talking a lot more and connecting with the other kids, and he seemed happy. Although he had not reached the milestones the other preschoolers had achieved, like holding a pencil firmly, drawing, emptying and filling containers, or climbing, he was a people person. Those milestones of developing a sense of humor and socializing meant that the other preschoolers and parents looked past the disability and saw Richard. Cute, sweet, funny, with a ready smile.

When Richard was five, I started the hunt for a primary school. I had been determined to send Richard to a Catholic primary school, but we found ourselves at the state primary school one suburb away from where we lived. It would become our other home and our other family for the next six years. I had exhausted all other possibilities: the local Catholic schools, our closer state primary school, and even a non-Catholic private boys' school where I had enrolled Richard not long after his birth. None of them worked for one reason or another. Usually the principal turned gray at the mere suggestion that he or she might have to enroll a child with Down syndrome: "How could we possibly cope with this alien in the classroom?" or "The funding just won't stretch" or "Perhaps you could find an alternative," blah blah blah.

I even had one parish priest pretty much tell me there was no hope for Richard in the world. I so badly wanted to slap him but thought better of it (although now I wish I did slap him). Underwhelmed by his lack of Christian compassion, I vowed that in the future I would be more cautious in my expectations of people I believed would be the ones to embrace us. Would I ever learn! I will be eternally grateful to the two principals who were happy to enroll Richard with a *Let's see how it goes* and *Let's give it a shot* attitude. Although I was keen for Rich to go to a private school—it kind of played into my vision of the "most successful son"—I knew deep down that it was not the right place. The second option was a much better choice. Both schools knew the value of inclusion and saw no barrier on account of Richard's intellectual capacity. He was a kid like everyone else and deserved an education like everyone else.

It was John Clegg of Mount Kuring-gai Primary School (MKPS) who won the day. Not only did he reassure us this was a school that promoted kindness and acceptance, but by the end of our interview with him he had made us feel we were doing him and the greater school community a favor by having Richard among them. Graeme and I could hardly believe our luck. Exclusion was only one breath, a word, away.

What a difference John made to our lives. Richard would now be attending a small, inclusive, mainstream school. It was close to a national park, had loads of space, and was safe. It would give Richard the start he needed. It's people like John Clegg who break down barriers by having the confidence to lead a staff and an entire community to accepting his vision. Before we knew it, we were running all of the wonderful back-to-school errands I had always dreamed of. Little things like buying school uniforms, shoes, backpacks, and lunch boxes had me in tears.

As much as we tried to prepare Richard for school, however, he still had some work to do on learning basic functions, like opening lunch boxes, zippers, and pencil cases. My biggest fear was toileting. He still had not mastered the art of pulling his pants up and down. Small things that most parents took for granted, we never could. His ability to perform most tasks was always a work in progress.

My frustration over this at times reached monumental heights, and as my anxiety increased, so did my nightmares. Like other kids with Down syndrome, Richard was smaller than his non–Down syndrome peers, and somewhat rounder. I had visions of his massive school backpack throwing him off-balance, leaving him lying in the school cafeteria like an upturned turtle with no one helping him and kids teasing him. I also had nightmares he would starve all day when no one would help him open his lunch box, or that he would wet his pants when no one would take him to the bathroom. It went on and on like this in the period leading up to the start of the term. Richard's vocabulary was good but his speech wasn't. Would the teachers and kids understand him? The poor boy was repeatedly asked to work through his speech therapy exercises. In part they were successful, but I wanted him to be as close to normal as possible. He—no, *we*—had to be accepted into the school community.

I was now working full-time, with Graeme being the stay-at-home dad and working on his business. We knew how important it was for Richard to have a parent at home. I was also lucky enough to have employers who were flexible and understood that, because of Richard's special education, I had to attend various school-related things. The closer we came to the first day of school, the more my anxiety levels grew, and I was spreading that anxiety to my family, including Richard, who announced he did not want to go to school anymore. He looked sad and incredibly vulnerable. What was I doing? What should have been an exciting time for all of us became difficult and scary, and it was my doing. I knew if I did not get my anxiety levels down, I would be jeopardizing this opportunity for a better life for him. During past periods of anxiety and depression, I had taken antidepressants and visited clairvoyants, faith healers, and Chinese herbalists. I prayed often and earnestly; I went to church. In the end, I found that meditation was my only real relief. I meditated day and night, and it fast became a way of life. Living close to a national park, I also took walks every day. A glass of wine or two with dinner was also very helpful. That first school day could not come fast enough. Finally, and to my great relief, it did.

As we approached the school, I felt my stomach in my throat. I think I must have asked Richard a hundred times if he was excited. Suddenly we were in the middle of the school playground surrounded by kids, parents, teachers—a cacophony. It was all a bit bewildering, and then a woman appeared out of nowhere with a big smile and red hair. "Hi, I'm Simone and this is Annette," she said. Her voice was full of warmth. "Her son is Harry and my son is Tom, and we have been looking for a Dick." I am sorry to say that at this moment my sense of humor failed me and I blurted out, "We only ever call him Richard. Nice to meet you. I am Benny and this is Graeme, and of course this is Richard."

"We are so thrilled Richard is here," Simone said. "He is in the same class as our boys, so welcome. The classroom is over there."

Here's how the redheaded Simone remembers that day, bless her:

I remembered Richard from the induction classes. There were two children who couldn't leave their parents' side, Richard and our Tom. All the other children went to the kindergarten class-room to do some craft and get to know each other, but not Tom and Richard. They stayed with us in the library. I was delighted when I saw that Richard was going to start at Mount Kuring-gai, because I knew that the lessons in life that he could teach us would be lessons that we couldn't learn in the classroom. He was an instantly likable child, and that's never changed.

Suddenly I felt so much better. We had friends. Nice people, lovely people. As we made our way toward the classroom, I could feel the tears well up. I felt hopeless. Knowing I should be happy, I tried so hard not to cry, not to fall apart, not to show Richard that I was sad. Even now, as I write this, tears are streaming down my face. Here was another bloody challenge; here we were jumping into another abyss. I was already sick of life's challenges, and this was one of the big ones.

"You must be Richard. Hello, Richard, I'm Mrs. Carragher, and I am your class teacher."

"Hello, Mrs. Carragher," Richard said. His voice was soft and sweet. By then my grip on him was so firm that I think he could sense Mum and Dad had to go. The floodgates opened. Tears streamed down my face, which started Richard off as well.

"Thanks, I'll take it from here," said Mrs. Carragher. And off they went, this very special teacher, who was more than equipped to inte-grate our son into a traditional classroom. Here's Karen Carragher:

I remember Benny giving a brief to the staff. It was an emotional episode for her rehashing the past [but] that was so helpful for me seeking support from other staff. Benny and Graeme weren't overly concerned with academic progress, more the social aspect and Richard's happiness. This suited me to the ground, as my teaching philosophy was/is the holistic approach of knocking out unsettling physical and emotional issues before expecting progress in learning. As with other students with intellectual disabilities who I've had in the classroom, because of their earlier years of support from therapy courses such as speech, occupational, and physio, their differences and ability to be part of the whole and in small group activities isn't restrictive until about year two onward.

In that first year, there were significant issues that needed to be dealt with, and we were so fortunate that Karen Carragher had the experience to ensure that all of Richard's needs were met. She managed the difficult and time-consuming tasks of getting Richard the help he needed in the bathroom—his hands still not strong enough to turn the taps—and using the playground equipment, and juggled many hats to make his early schooling as enjoyable and useful as possible.

At times I felt we had no right to ask the school for additional one-on-one hours, even though we felt Richard needed more. That's what happens, of course: you are grateful to be there, so you don't rock the boat. I have been critical of parents who do rock the boat and make a fuss. I don't think it achieves very much, apart from alienating teachers, who are the people you want most to help. But it is a difficult but necessary conversation to have: How can parents effectively advocate for their children? And, if need be, rock the boat without capsizing it?

There are no easy answers to these questions. Luckily, Mount Kuring-gai was exemplary in terms of staff, administration, and student body. Above all else, the students were taught to be good people. The following is a fine example from Richard's friend Tom of what sort of school we had found. It made me laugh so much too:

We never had any fights at school. It was how the school was. I remember that when I went to high school, I didn't realize that you could tease people for being redheads. We never teased James for his red hair. Us kids were just never in that environment because our parents were never like that. I think it was fortunate that MKPS was a very small school as well. We knew to a degree that

Richard was different, but he was always so nice. I remember one kid would take everyone's trains, and no one wanted to be around him. But you knew if you wanted to play a game with someone, Richard was always happy to share.

Most of the kids at MKPS were totally fine having Richard at the school. They did not see any difference to start with, and when they did, their acceptance was already there. They all grew together, which is what happens when we bring together the able and the disabled. Repugnant words like "retard" and "spaz" never even enter the picture.

As I said, Graeme and I did not make demands, but the school eventually did. They demanded help from the Department of Education to provide Richard with the help he needed. It was not easy for them, as he had been progressing well, and the better he did, the less money there was for more hours with a teacher's aide to keep up with the pace. It's weird, isn't it: having to fight for something that should be encouraged? It presents you with some difficult options, as Karen Carragher shows in this recollection of one of our meetings that year:

There was a meeting halfway through the year with several people, including Benny, Graeme, and myself, to reapply for a teacher's aide allocation of more hours. All of his life to date, Benny and Graham had strived for Rich to achieve to the best of his ability. In an assessment by another teacher, Richard came out as "lower" in need, and it was explained to us his allocation would be reduced because of this. We needed the allocation to at least remain the same because it was working. So there we all were, and instead of looking at the positives in Richard's development, Benny, Graeme, and I were made to look for negatives. I remember Benny and Graeme's faces, and it gutted me.

Over the years at MKPS, we cultivated friendships, had good support where it counted, and generally were accepted. Most families had no issues with Richard being at the school, but one or two did, as my friend Carolyn recalls:

> Reactions from the parents at Mount Kuring-gai while Richard was there were mainly positive, although one parent decided Richard was not eligible to attend her son's birthday party because the other kids may not have known how to include him. Truthfully, I think the problem lay more with the mother than the invitees, but there's one in every school. Many people don't agree with "special" children attending mainstream schools, but unless you walk in our shoes, it's probably best not to voice an opinion. It's hard enough to source the best options, let alone choose the appropriate one that gives our child the best possible outcome.

Many years later, that parent who did not want Richard at her son's party was standing behind me at the local supermarket checkout. My trolley was full to overflowing; she was carrying a carton of milk and bread. Usually I would just say to that person, "Please go before me, as I have a lot," but on that day all I could think about was that she didn't invite Richard to her son's party. Childishly and smugly, I turned, looked her in the eye, and then turned my back to her and took a very long time to unpack my trolley. I know I shouldn't have . . . but it felt good to get one back.

As with any area of life, be it school, workplace, sports team, or neighborhood, it is impossible for all relationships to go smoothly, but for the most part this was a rewarding and beneficial time of our lives. We took part in school life. I volunteered for reading and canteen duties. Graeme did school maintenance and was always the go-to parent for anything else. We had some terrific friends, like Louise, the mother of James:

> I recall that first meeting so clearly. I felt a flood of emotions when I saw Richard. I had an awkward moment of not knowing

exactly what to say as I tried to suppress my surprise, sadness, pity, confusion, and overwhelming curiosity to understand more. My scientific background went into analyzing the likelihood of having a Down syndrome child at the age of thirty. I was curious to know if Richard had siblings; I wondered how Benny and Graeme coped and what the impact of Richard was on their lives. I also questioned how Richard would settle into a regular classroom, what additional support would be required, and how that of course might affect my son James and his classmates. I had chosen Mount Kuring-gai because it was smaller than other schools in the area; I think it was a little over 150 students at the time. I was hoping for a close community with a strong sense of support, free of any bullying. I'm sure Benny and Graeme had similar expectations. At that moment, I felt an immediate sadness for Richard; he was so small and appeared so vulnerable. Would the school have the resources to protect, support, and respond to his daily needs?

I can say, regarding my educational concerns, I need not have worried. I now understand the diversity that exists in every classroom. I believe the inclusion of Richard at MKPS provided us all, but more importantly our children, with a special life lesson. Learning with someone (usually) less able than themselves gave our children a chance to learn a little bit about tolerance. I'm sure there were good and bad times. However, in my view, James and the others approached Richard in pretty much the same way as any other kid—although occasionally he did get some special attention from the more nurturing classmates.

As Richard grew older, his schooling became easier. There were some awkward times, some scary times, and oceans of fun times. Richard won "Aussie of the Year" one month and was so proud. He went on many school excursions, as all the other kids did. Families came and went; relationships blossomed and fizzled. He took part in school carnivals, where he was often given a head start and sometimes encouraged to win. At such times his difference stood out, and although I appreciated the generous spirit with which it was intended, I was often left feeling vulnerable and lonely. Maybe it was self-pity. I was conflicted between the joy of Richard's success and the burden of maintaining the façade of happiness. The restrictions of his disability, the high standard I expected, and just the sheer weight of the unknown future had me in a dark place.

Life also had its funny moments. I find it interesting that many people assume that if someone has an intellectual disability, they lack a sense of humor. I wonder if it is expected that just because you may be incapable of winning a Mensa prize, wit is above and beyond you. In any case, Richard has always been the exception to that rule.

One afternoon I was in a supermarket with Richard when we noticed a girl about Richard's age in the same aisle as us. She had an obvious disability. She was nonverbal and was making wild gestures with her arms, all the while staring at Richard. Bewildered, he turned to me.

"What the hell is she staring at, Mum?"

I didn't mean to, but I started laughing. The fact that he saw himself as being like everyone else and was confounded by her stare—and that he saw her as the one with the problem—was a funny moment. At about the age of seven, Richard had begun to develop his own brand of humor. He saw the world through his eyes—not mine; not Graeme's; just his—and the world was just plain funny to him. He laughed a lot, and he knew how to make people laugh.

One of my greatest joys is Richard's rich vocabulary. He gets words; he understands their power. He also screws them up, sometimes intentionally, sometimes not.

"Mum, I have an itchy tentacle."

"What? A tentacle? What's a tentacle?"

"You know, like an octopus."

"But you don't have tentacles."

"Yes I do."

"Where are your tentacles?"

"Between my legs."

"No, you dill! It's testicles."

"No it's not, they're tentacles."

"When did you start calling them tentacles?"

"I've always called them tentacles."

Sometimes he'd drive me mad with incessant questions. We'd be at a traffic light, and I would politely wave someone in to my lane.

"Who's that?"

"I don't know; I just let them in."

"But you waved to them."

"Yes, just to let them into the lane."

"So you do know them?"

"No, I don't know them."

"But you waved at them."

As he got older, he would carry on like this just to piss me off. He'd give me a look that said, "Gotcha!" He loved to sing along with ABBA, and his favorite line was "Yes, I've been brokenhearted / Blue since the day we FARTED." Word games and rhyming were important for his word-building skills. Graeme was very good at this, and Richard loved it.

❧

As time went on, however, my anxiety went into a new phase. I would worry that I would die or, even worse, that Richard would. I had always been a terrible hypochondriac, but it was now getting ridiculous. A headache was a brain tumor, a cut was bound to become gangrenous, and a tummy ache meant a twisted bowel. Death or illness was always present.

Richard's circle grew smaller and smaller as he and his friends got older, and from about the age of ten his difference became more pronounced. He was rarely invited to parties, on playdates, or for sleepovers. I was sad this was happening but not entirely surprised, as I had expected the honeymoon to end a lot sooner. However, little girls in particular went well beyond the call of duty in looking out for Richard. They often mothered him. Much to his great relief, they would often do things for him, which eventually became an expectation on his part. He relished that great power he had. Although at the time I felt it was perhaps damaging for him, I think that kindness made Richard appreciate that he had the charm and sweetness that is still evident today and that he still uses.

When those gorgeous girls moved on, as of course they had to, Richard's loneliness became evident. He could see that everything was changing. It's not that he was in any way shunned; the kids simply divided into groups that often didn't include him. The boys grew bigger, louder, and stronger, and Richard just couldn't keep up. He did have one lovely friend, Harry, who invited him over regularly. That friendship was special for Richard. It made him feel important.

Throughout all this, differences in how Graeme and I approached life finally came to a head, and our relationship ended after seventeen years. I was ambitious, restless, and striving for much more, whereas Graeme's approach was much more laid-back and quiet. He was happy to just live a plain, simple life, didn't particularly want to socialize with people, and was happy to keep just the three of us and the dog at home. I was in a totally different place. The more Richard grew, the more I wanted people in our lives. I was bored in suburban Sydney and wanted Richard to see more of the world. I felt I was drowning in a sea of mediocrity.

It was awful for all of us, but the ever-resilient Richard was circumspect in his attitude. He knew neither of us was truly happy and he would comment on it. I tried hard to protect him from problems, but he was like a little sponge, taking in our highs and lows. Because Graeme was the stay-at-home parent and I was at work, the transition wasn't too horrible. But of course I read it that way because it made me feel better about what had happened. I felt less guilt, certainly. Marriage breakdown affects everyone: children, extended family, and friends—even the family mutt. There are consequences if you stay and there are consequences if you leave. Neither of us was truly happy with the parting, but we were different people, with different expectations. It is not for me to write about how Graeme felt; this was his private life and I respect that. As for me, I thought it best we go our separate ways while we were young enough (I was thirty-seven and Graeme was forty-one) to perhaps start again. So I made that decision not lightly but with a truly heavy heart. I was only too conscious that Richard already had enough difficulties in life without divorced parents as well.

My concern was that Richard would have a stable home and school life and continue with everything he normally did. His resourceful radar detected that things were not well between his parents. It did not come as a shock to him when we sat down with him and broke our news. In fact, he had once said to me, "Mum, I know you and Dad are unhappy. You should move out."

I was stunned by his ability to pick up on things I had thought he would never notice.

I did as he advised.

# Planes, Trains, and Automobiles

"Why do you go away? So that you can come back. So that you can see the place you came from with new eyes and extra colors. And the people there see you differently, too. Coming back to where you started is not the same as never leaving."

—TERRY PRATCHETT, *A HAT FULL OF SKY*

"Are we there yet? Are we there yet?"

"No, Richard, we are not there yet, and if you ask me one more time, I am going to pull over and leave you by the side of the road."

One of the huge differences between Graeme and me was his love of staying home and my love of not staying home, whether that meant overseas travel or somewhere closer. By the time I was twenty-five, I had lived in the UK and traveled several times through Europe, so I always had itchy feet. Graeme had traveled as well, but now he was done. He was happiest at home. So I would often grab Richard for a weekend drive. He, along with the dog, loved going somewhere—anywhere. It meant a new adventure, a new place to see, new people to meet. It could also mean a treat or a nice lunch somewhere. I really wanted Richard to like travel, to see the world, and not just from my perspective. I did not want his world to feel narrow. Although he was only eight years old, I wanted him to really "feel" life.

It started with an innocent flight to Brisbane to see my auntie

Doris and uncle Tony. They had been begging me for ages to bring Richard up to see them. There was an abundance of kisses and hugs, and they had made sure that whenever they saw Richard they gave him a gold coin or two for his money box. The last time they'd seen Richard, they proudly produced a $2 gold coin. By this stage Richard had worked out that some money was worth more than others.

"Now, Richard, darling, here is a two-dollar coin for your money box."

"Thanks, Auntie Doris, but I would prefer paper money."

We had all missed Auntie Doris and Uncle Tony when they moved up north, so the trip was exciting for us both. I was also putting my big toe into the travel water to see how Richard managed with flight. He had sensitive ears. Children with Down syndrome often have ear issues due to the smallness of their eustachian tubes; a eustachian tube connects the middle ear to the nose. Too much noise hurt him. He had totally freaked when I took him to a Wiggles concert a year earlier, so how he would cope with airplane noise was anyone's guess. Only time (and a possibly wretched experience) would tell.

As an eight-year-old, Richard was still finding his feet. Literally. His balance was not great and there were still issues with his mobility and speech. I was therefore nervous. Having traveled on business for many years, however, I was well aware of the drill. At the check-in counter the staff could not have been nicer, and once on the plane my little man was getting way too much attention from the crew. He, of course, lapped it up. The engines started up. His fingers tightly gripped my hand and he went into talk overdrive and proceeded to talk the entire ninety-minute journey to Brisbane. No respite.

"What's that cloud doing?"

"It's a cloud, honey; it's in the sky to make shade and rain and for birds to sit on." (I'm no scientist, so give me a break.)

"What happens if we bump into it?"

"Nothing. We just go through it."

"Will it hurt us?"

"No, it won't hurt us."

"How much longer to go?"

"About another hour and a half. Would you like me to read you a book?"

"So, what if a bird hits the cloud?"

It was far too early for a drink.

He loved every minute of it. He loved the excitement, the people, and the possibilities that travel brings. After our time with my aunt and uncle, we headed home. Same deal with the clouds and the birds, but this time he was calmer. He knew the drill now.

"Where will we go next time, Mum?"

"How about a road trip?"

So began Richard's travel bug.

At this time I rented a rather funny little house not too far away from Graeme with the idea we would share custody week on and week off. It worked for a while. Then, as I was trying to juggle work, traveling long distances, and seeing Richard, a new man came into my life. Foolishly, I went into this new relationship much too quickly, swept away as I was with the romance and the excitement.

Initially, Richard was excited to have two homes. He was having a relatively happy time at his school and wasn't too concerned about the change of lifestyle. I can justify anything when I want to, and I did. How could I have expected this little person to understand the complexities of his mother's situation and just accept that this was now his new life? Yet he did—almost. From a young age Richard has always shown a deep understanding of human nature. I am not entirely sure how it developed or if Graeme and I nurtured it, but it is very real. It's like a built-in radar that allows him to notice the slightest change happening around him. He often preempts conversations I've barely considered having with him. It's a bit spooky and often catches me off guard. He knows when I am hurt or distressed and gives me more hugs than usual. When I was going through the change from our old life to our new one, he was more enthusiastic than usual about any activity we did. He would delight in telling my friends that he now had two homes, with two beds, two PlayStations, two of everything. He liked my new partner, but I could see that he was not really 100 percent comfortable. Who was this new man with his mum?

My partner and I married in 2000 and moved from the suburbs of Sydney to the inner city, with more travel, dinner parties, theater, and a lot more entertaining. We had only known each other a short period of time. I had moved into a new role with a multinational publishing house, and he had been sent over from the head office in the UK to oversee some management changes. He was living in New Zealand, so it was easy for him to transition to Australia. We were the same age and shared a passion for books and travel. He was charming and "frightfully" English. Although it never occurred to me that being a single mum with a child with Down syndrome could put many suitors off, it was apparent that people thought this man was a saint for taking on a woman with an intellectually disabled son. People asked me if he knew what he was getting himself into. Did he know anything about intellectual disability? This is the attitude that saw Richard as a burden.

As for me, I thought my partner was lucky to have us. I thought he did too. With marriage came a gorgeous little stepson and a stepbrother for Richard. Even though my partner's son lived in New Zealand with his mother, we tried to ensure we had plenty of visits and holidays together. It was not an easy time. The boys were total opposites and it was hard for them both, but much harder for my stepson with his dad so far from home. The boys tried their best, but during these early visits each clung to their biological parent. We all managed, but I am sure we could have done better.

People were coming and going, new business ventures opened, and I was feeling pretty good about everything. Being closer to the city again, I was enjoying retail therapy more than ever. New hairstyle, smarter clothes; I even started doing my nails! Richard enjoyed seeing more of my family. His cousins were in and out and would babysit him often. He loved that part of inner-city living and he could see his mum was happier. In hindsight, I wish I had not embraced this life-style so exuberantly. I thought Richard would adjust well. But it soon became clear it was unworkable. I made the decision that sharing custody from a distance was not smart, and both he and I would become exhausted with the travel involved. Graeme and I came to a decision that Rich would come to me most weekends and maybe one night in the week. The rest of the time he would be with his dad. But I had not discussed this fully with Richard.

One important aspect of Richard's outlook is that if he knows you are clear about why you are doing something or why plans change, he will work with you happily to move forward. But—and it's a huge but—if you are not fully in tune with his needs or his need for clarity, then there is an almighty struggle. His stubbornness is something to grapple with. When it's on, it's really on, and no amount of cajoling, bribing, or threats will move him into your corner. When Richard was little, there were times I would be at my breaking point, and he would sit down on the ground and refuse to move. He did this to me once in the women's section of a fancy department store. He just sat down and rendered himself a complete deadweight. I was so frustrated with him that I sat down behind him and pushed him along with my feet. He still wouldn't budge. By then I'd drawn a crowd, so with all my strength I got up, grabbed both his arms, and said, "If you don't get up, I am going to leave you here forever and no one will feed you." That worked, but I was rather embarrassed, and he couldn't have cared less.

That stubbornness and difficult behavior started to become more apparent. He wanted to embrace the change, but he was not entirely comfortable with it. Why would he be? His world had been turned upside down in only a very short period of time. We all had to try to adjust. But the more I read, the more I realized that it is not really a "stubbornness"—it's more what is called "grooves." There are set patterns (call them routines in his actions and thoughts) that just don't like to be broken. It was scary for Richard to do things that would break his "groove" and his mother was pushing all his "grooves'" patterns.

Being in the throes of a new relationship, I tried to bring as many aspects of my life together as possible. New man, new home, new job, as I was now building a publishing company. It wasn't perfect, but somehow it all seemed to work. I was busy with all this and assumed that Richard would be lonely and needing some stability, so I called in the troops. My nieces, Carly and Melanie, and their younger sister Faith had created a special bond with Richard. They had fought over him from the day he was born: who got to hold him, who could wash him, who played with him. They would travel the length of Sydney to see him and bring their school friends too. They wanted to show him off; they were proud of him, and although they knew that Richard was different and always would be, they set about ensuring that their relationship with him would be separate from the relationship they had with me. Melanie, now a mum of four, expresses that relationship perfectly:

Richard is important to me. He is important to me because of the adventures we have shared. The jokes we have laughed. The way we both value and cherish our family. Richard has Down syndrome. He also has a giant heart, a great sense of humor, a sweet tooth, and the worst singing voice you ever did hear.

They built something more than just a family bond. They built something so profound that his disability was never an obstacle in the way they communicated or loved him. This taught Richard to be ever more resilient as they introduced him to the excitement of inner-city living. The girls would take Richard with them to the footy, the beach, amusement parks, and other events. He was their cousin, and they believed that, like everyone else, he should enjoy life. Richard's development came on in spades; his language improved and his sense of humor expanded. There were no barriers; everything was possible for him.

By now my partner's career was taking him to all corners of the globe, and suddenly he was assigned to New York City for no particular length of time, but I thought no more than twelve months. Should I stay or should I go? I was newly married and excited at the prospect of living in New York. We were now building a business of our own and doing it in the most powerful city in the world. It looked like an opportunity too good to miss. I could say that I had second thoughts about this, that I was worried about the impact it would have on Richard, but that wouldn't be true. I was very excited and didn't foresee that I would be judged any more harshly than a man making a similar decision. I thought that if this stint were only for a short period of time, it would be manageable. We had plenty of frequent-flier points and I could jet back and forth often to spend time with Richard and my family. I knew I would miss him and he would miss me, but I knew he'd be safe and loved with Graeme.

I chose to go, blindly thinking it wouldn't be that difficult.

But it was. I can't say that I didn't have a fabulous time in Manhattan, but there was always that niggling doubt: Had I given my motherhood away for the bright lights? Every time I boarded a plane back to Sydney, I felt I should stay there with Richard and not return to my partner. In the seven months that I lived in New York City, I traveled back to Australia three times. It was exhausting but it was also wonderful seeing my son. We spent time with my family and friends, catching up on daily lives, focusing on Richard, ensuring that he knew his mother well. I worried that he might become alienated from me. In the trips back and forth, through hours of endless skies, I tried to make sense of this life and what the future would hold.

In fact, we were both torn—torn between two little boys, Richard and my partner's son. It was 2001, and we planned to leave New York in September and head back to New Zealand. My partner's life to date had been so peripatetic; he now felt it was time to live closer to his nine-year-old boy. I was thinking that after a time Richard would come and join us there.

But we suddenly found ourselves in a city under attack, and we couldn't get out. It was September 11. We lived on West Eleventh Street, perhaps a fifteen- or twenty-minute walk to the World Trade Center, where we had breakfasted the previous Sunday. On that brilliantly sunny morning I was having a coffee, preparing for a day uptown, meeting New York publishers about our little antipodean publishing company. One thing you never hear in New York is the sound of airplanes, so I became concerned when our building started to shake. I had an awful feeling that something dreadful was happening when I heard an almighty bang. We were close to the Hudson. Had a plane crashed into the river? I ran into the living room, turned the TV on, and saw what was happening a close distance away. It was all too horrendous and too much to comprehend. My partner was already uptown, so I called him. As we were talking, the second plane hit.

"Okay," he said. "This is not an accident; it's a terrorist attack. Stay put. Don't go out and I will be back as soon as I can."

"All right," I said.

Then the phone went dead.

But the Internet was working. Frantic emails were sent very quickly to Graeme, my sisters, and my partner's family to tell them we were alive. Clearly many were not. What I didn't want to happen was for ten-year-old Richard to be told by someone that buildings had fallen down in New York. My thoughts were racing. How could this have happened? What was going on?

A girlfriend from Melbourne was up late watching the news unfold, so she called me. Yes, I assured her, we were safe. And the phone worked, yes. Perhaps I could get through to Graeme. *Tell Richard I love him.* The phone went dead for a second time and stayed dead for many days.

Thankfully, my partner returned to the apartment later that day.

We still had power. I was transfixed by the images on the TV as I hoped and prayed someone would come out alive. Then the emails started arriving from concerned friends and relatives all over the globe. I sent Richard emails assuring him I was okay, telling him I loved him and that I was safe. The smell of burning plastic permeated our apartment. Because of our proximity to the World Trade Center, we were in lockdown and could not leave our neighborhood without showing our passports. An eerie silence pervaded the city, broken only by wailing sirens. Sheets of paper showing the faces of missing people were posted all over buildings in the area, pleading with survivors to help locate them.

I just wanted to go home, but to get out we had to go by train to Toronto, which we did. From there we headed to Scotland to see my partner's family. This was an arrangement that had already been in place well before the events in New York. By now I was really missing Richard. But home was not going to be back in Sydney, of course, but in Auckland.

To this day I have no idea why I agreed to this plan. It seemed to make sense at the time. It was decided that Richard would come over for holidays, or I would go to him in Sydney, especially if there was a school activity or event. Since it was only a three-hour flight, I went back and forth many times in that first year, but I desperately wanted Richard to be with me. He was changing. He was now ten and he had, in a short period of time, grown up, and I felt I was missing this.

❧

Accepting that Richard was never going to be Einstein was one thing, but it didn't mean there wasn't still work to do as far as his education went. On my trips back, language was always an issue. Sometimes his words were incoherent, so I would make him repeat them over and over until he got them right. Poor kid. We usually practiced in the car, which was such a great place for the two of us to just be together, to talk and sing and laugh. If a word didn't sound right or his grammar was incorrect, we'd work on it. Half an hour later I would ask him to say "presume" again and he would say "pessume" as if we had never worked on it. Sometimes he got it wrong on purpose, just to annoy me, and other times it was truly beyond his grasp and he would argue.

"But I'm right, Mum."

"No you're not."

"Yes I am."

Sometimes he won; sometimes I did.

"Woolingone."

"No, it's Wollongong."

"That's what I am saying."

"No you're not. You're saying Woolingone."

"Yes, that's right."

I have to say, my own vocabulary and diction left a lot to be desired, but I would not allow Richard to be lazy with his pronunciation.

"Sorry, what did you just say?"

"Prdon."

"Richard, I have told you a million times it's *par*-don. Pardon."

With that menace in his eye, he'd reply, "Pardon, pardon, feel better now?"

My son could sometimes give as good as he got.

Auckland was not a hugely exciting city. For me, back then, it had very little going for it other than the place we lived, which was a delightful community called Titirangi. It means "fringe of heaven" in Maori, and it felt like that at times, with its lush canopy of old-growth kauri trees and an abundance of pohutukawa, the colorful New Zealand Christmas tree. The house was perched on a cliff with stunning views across Manukau Harbor.

It was not, however, Greenwich Village. Relocating from the most exciting city in the world to one that at the time was quite dull was, to say the least, difficult. Even more so was being so close to Richard, my family, and my friends yet still so far away. Friends are harder to come by as you age, and isolation is an issue when you work from home. Building the publishing house from the bottom of the world was grueling but fun, and at least I got to talk to booksellers and other people besides my husband. Socializing was enjoyable but provided no real sense of belonging. I felt like an outsider most of the time, and I was missing my home. Trips across the ditch became more frequent. I wanted to see Richard.

On those visits home, I would pick Rich up from his dad's and we would either drive to some accommodation or to my mother's or sisters' houses. We would often have to share a bed. He loved snuggling up and being read to. He wanted to be told stories of his early childhood, of what life was like before he had a memory. What plans did I have for the time we had together? When he slept, I would just look at him in the dim bedside light. He always looked so peaceful, so content. I would watch his breathing, touch his face or his arm, or tighten the blanket to ensure he was warm enough. These things, these precious moments of our time, mother-and-son time, helped me through those periods of isolation. I imprinted those images in my memory so that I could conjure them up as needed.

Living with Graeme full-time meant that Richard was getting to know Lorraine, Graeme's partner, and her boys, Justin and Max. They seemed like good kids and Lorraine was lovely with Richard. As a mum, you worry about the "wicked stepmother," but I didn't have a worry when it came to Lorraine. She took care of Richard with kindness and support. I was glad for Richard to have siblings. They could teach him how to be less selfish, to share and to connect.

I am not sure how easy it was for Richard to share his father or indeed his mother. On the surface he was generous and diplomatic about his feelings regarding his new life with his new families. Underneath his brave façade, though, I knew Richard had issues in trying to adjust, trying to work out how he fitted into this new world, his dad's and mine. It was a lot to ask of him, but Lorraine helped a great deal with that. She recalls:

As time went by and Richard's dad and I started a relationship, Richard became an integral part of my life and family. The five of us (Graeme and I and Richard and my two sons) spent a lot of time together as a family unit: going on holidays, enjoying weekends together, and generally doing the everyday stuff that kids and families do. None of us ever treated Richard as someone with a disability. He was just one of the boys, and although he was given some extra consideration and care and encouragement at times, it was never made obvious. It was wonderful to watch Justin and Max cheering him on in the pool when he was learning to swim, and he has ended up being the best swimmer in our family. Richard was always kind and thoughtful—he remembered all the birthdays, all the special occasions for everyone, and was constantly keen to celebrate: "Maybe we could go out for dinner?" He was concerned whenever one of us was sick or injured. His first thought was to inquire, "How are you feeling today?" and "Are you feeling better?"

As for Graeme, he was and still is a terrific father. He adores Richard and brings out the best in him. Graeme is always in the moment with Richard, and their relationship remained rock solid even during those difficult years. As Graeme says:

On reflection, the time I spent as a single dad with Richard did more for him than I could have imagined. With the various dramas of the previous few years, I think he gained a lot of self-assurance knowing that I needed him as much as he needed me. Being a male parent, I'll admit to being a little lax in terms of responsibility, which meant that Richard was inadvertently forced to come to the fore a little more often than would otherwise have been the case. All these years later he still thrives on organizing and taking responsibility for everything, to the degree that I'll often have to tell him to lighten up. "It's not your problem," I'll say.

After three years of traveling back and forth between Auckland and Sydney to see him, I wanted Rich to come and live with me, and he said he wanted to. But Graeme was totally opposed to him moving. It was a bitter time, but in hindsight the better decision was made. Richard stayed put. Lorraine and Graeme's life was stable. They were still living in the family home, which was comfortable for them both. My life was still built around my career, the business, and a lot of travel.

But eventually I cracked. Depression had set in once again. My second marriage was not in a good place. I was acutely aware that it was not just Richard I had to think about but also my stepson. I wanted to go home, but that would mean big changes for him. I wasn't sure if my partner wanted to leave his beloved Titirangi, but I knew I couldn't stay there any longer. Richard would begin high school soon, and I wanted to be as close to him as I could. My partner believed our marriage was worth working on and so was willing to compromise and be a long-distance father as long as we settled somewhere rural.

So back to Australia we went.

# 6

# A Cup Half-Full

"The people are immensely likable—cheerful, extrovert, quick-witted, and unfailingly obliging . . . They have a society that is prosperous, well ordered, and instinctively egalitarian. Life doesn't get much better than this."
—BILL BRYSON, *IN A SUNBURNED COUNTRY*

It felt good to be home. From the moment I arrived in Wollombi, I fell in love with the place. It was an hour and fifteen minutes away from Graeme's house, where Richard, now thirteen, was living full-time, but quite a way from my family, who were about two and a half hours away in "the Shire." I had missed them and the comforts of familiarity. I had missed watching my nieces and nephew grow and regretted that Richard had not seen them very often during the years I lived abroad. I could now look forward to making new memories with all of them in this new, wild paradise. I had missed Australia; I had especially missed the light, the color of that familiar blue sky.

Richard was overjoyed to have me home. "I love you so much, Mum. I am so happy."

And he was. Connecting with him again, I felt hopeful that I could undo all the hurt I had caused him. Self-judgment was not helpful, and I decided to leave the past as just that: the past. Others were not so generous. The occasional snide remark about living overseas or abandoning my son was not helpful. All I cared about was that I could finally see, hold, love, and mother my son all I wanted.

The village of Wollombi was an interesting place. The families who had lived there for generations were farmers. Arriving later were the hippies, musicians, actors, and Sydney refugees. When we arrived, so did many corporate types from Sydney, including a lot of weekenders. Some small villages won't consider you a local until you've been there for at least ten years, but Wollombi embraced us as soon as we walked into the tavern. The natural beauty of the valley is beguiling. You notice it immediately, but it takes a few years to really see it. The power of ancient Aboriginal culture is everywhere. On my many walks into the bush, I could feel the presence of all the people who had come there before me. It was quite humbling and a truly blessed experience.

The property we bought was on one hundred acres with two dwellings and a few outhouses. It comprised a large five-bedroom house and a two-bedroom cottage that would eventually house our business. The main house was roomy and comfortable, but it took me some time to adjust to rural living: to the tank water, the regular power and phone outages, no mobile phone reception, floods, droughts, rodents, and—my least favorite—snakes. There were black ones, brown ones, green ones, and they could all kill. There is something very unnerving knowing you can walk within an inch of one of the deadliest snakes in the world without realizing it. How would Richard's reflexes deal with this? How would my nerves?

We set about creating a warm and open home for family and friends to visit on a regular basis. My father was the first to fall in love with Wollombi. The farmer and gardener in him was enraptured by it and took the chance to be there as often as he could. My mother, on the other hand, missed us being close. "Why can't you just be like the rest of us and live in the city?" she said during their first visit.

Richard loved our new home, although I'm not sure if he truly loved the property or if it was that he was seeing more of me. I like to think it was the latter. He had grown and was flourishing. He was now thirteen years and starting to show more "maleness." He was sprouting chest hair, his voice deepened, and even his limbs became thicker and hairy. It alarmed me. No longer a little boy, he was turning into a teenager. Yikes. I was unsure how this village would embrace a young man with Down syndrome. It is always such an unknown. I knew I could fit in and become part of the community, but what would they think of Richard? We started with little steps. A trip to the town center, an introduction here, a family history told to a neighbor. The tavern was a great place to meet, and as people got to know us, they got to know Richard. For him, getting to know Wollombi meant getting to know the people. There was a bond, this feeling that we lived in a special place with some special people. That specialness of place was never more evident than in the way Richard was embraced and accepted. He became something of a local celebrity.

"How ya goin', mate?"

"Ya mum looking after you, mate?"

"Richie, good to see you again. Would you like a lemonade? A wine for your mum?"

Small communities like this are built around the passions and interests of their residents. In Wollombi, you could volunteer to join any number of groups: the historic society; the Valley Artists; the Chamber of Commerce; the Progress Association; a tennis, garden, or pony club; the volunteer fire brigade; St. Michael the Archangel's Wollombi (Catholic) Church; or St. John's Anglican Church. You could join Pilates or yoga or meditation classes or hang out with the creative women at the Stitch and Bitch. All this in a community with only about three hundred people on the electoral roll. Old families and new joined these groups.

We were starting a new chapter. Being so much closer to Richard was now possible. I knew I could not have him with me all the time, but having him on weekends, school holidays, and sometimes midweek was a blessing. Being able to drive to him, go to the movies, go shopping, or go bowling was now all possible. For the first time in years, I was able to be a proper school mum.

Not long after we moved in, I had a surprise for Richard. It was a bright autumn morning, and the sky was clearest blue. Having Rich with me seemed to make things exciting and so much more fun.

"After breakfast, we are going for a drive. I have a surprise for you."

"A surprise? What's the surprise?"

"We are going for a ten-minute drive to pick up two puppies."

"Two? Two, Mum? Will they bite me?"

"No, they are puppies. Aren't you excited?"

I so wanted to share this with him, as I think I really wanted him to be as excited as I was about having puppies on the property. But I could see the uncertainty in his eyes. This was and still is a thing with Richard. He really loves the idea of something, but then the reality of it sends him into a total spin. He wants to be excited, but his own safety and well-being become his focus. Although he'd known Comet, the family dog, it had been some time since he had died; and although he had been around other dogs, he was frightened when they jumped on him. For all his optimism and joy of life, caution was always front of mind. Perhaps this was because of the natural fear that I projected onto him, which was very likely instilled by the language we often used to protect and shield him. I would often say to Richard "Watch out for this," "Mind where you are walking," "Don't speak to strangers," "Be careful of that."

Arriving at the farm, we were greeted by not just three or four puppies but eleven eight-week-old pups from which we had to choose just two. All these little baby kelpies, most of them brown, most yapping hysterically with tails wagging, were completely and adorably out of control. The owner, Emma, opened the gate for us to enter. Immediately, two little hands tightly clutched my arm.

"I don't want to go in, Mum."

"Oh, come on, Richard, they're just puppies, and you get to pick."

"But the mother dog there is looking at me. She might bite."

Taking this cue, Emma took over and said she would only bring out a few puppies at a time. I had already told her I was interested in two boy puppies. Out of all the brown puppies, there was one that was a tanned gold. He was very cute, and I picked him up.

"Look, Richard, what do you think of this one?"

He gave it a quick pat and seemed a little more relaxed. Unfortunately, at about the same time, the rest of the puppies came bounding out through an unclosed gate. Four-legged furry chaos reigned, and Richard's last semblance of composure disappeared. He completely freaked out and was almost climbing on top of me.

This is where I came undone. It's situations like this where that impatience of mine tends to raise its ugly head.

"Oh, for God's sake, Richard, don't be so stupid. They are just puppies; they're not going to hurt you. This is meant to be fun, so get your act together."

Well, that didn't work. His grip on me got even tighter, and he began to shout fearfully. Amid the confusion, one puppy latched onto my trouser leg. He was the biggest of the lot. I handed the tan puppy back to Emma, then tried to dislodge the big puppy from my trousers and detach Richard from my arm, but was unable to do either.

"Oh, for crying out loud, Rich, get in the car."

Emma suggested I spend just a few minutes more in the enclosure with them. I had almost decided that the little tan kelpie would come home with us. Emma had told us how placid and sweet-natured he was, and he appeared very content in my arms. I agreed but I really wanted two, so we had to decide on another.

Back in the safety of the car, Richard was acting a lot calmer. I walked over to him, the tan kelpie snuggled tightly against my chest.

"Do you think we should take this one home?"

"Yes, he is very cute," he said. And then he smiled.

I carefully handed him the puppy through the open car window, hoping that the enclosed space would be the best place for an introduction. Both took an instant liking to each other. The puppy sat on

Richard's lap, and he was happy as well as a little cautious. Then the puppy gave him a sloppy kiss.

"Okay, which one of you will also come home with us?" I asked as I entered the enclosure again. Again the larger puppy went straight for my trousers. He was now firmly attached, and as hard as I tried to play with the others, he was determined to get my attention.

"Mum, he wants to come home with you," Richard called out from the car. "Bring him home, Mum."

And we did, although I questioned that decision when halfway there the larger puppy vomited all over Richard's lap. The smell was disgusting, but country roads being what they were, there was no room to pull over. We both had to just put up with it.

"Sorry, mate," I told Richard, "you're just going to have to sit there till we get home."

Richard sat with the two puppies jumping all over him and vomit flying. Looking in the rearview mirror, I could see his face alternating between terror and delight. This was the beginning of a beautiful relationship between Richard and our dogs, Winston and Nero.

It was also the beginning of our renewed life as churchgoers. Although I had promised God I would go to church regularly, I had become a little bit lazy about attending weekly, but I assumed God would understand how busy my life had become. We joined our local Catholic church. You expect that a little country church would not have many attendees, and that was just how it was with this one. Although I worried about being accepted, there was no need: The parishioners were loving and embracing, and we immediately felt part of the congregation. What I didn't expect to find in our little church in this tiny community were another mother and child with Down syndrome. What were the chances? This was odd, very odd, but good, very good. *This is clearly okay,* I thought. *This little village is familiar with Down syndrome; barriers have already been broken. No need to explain anything. Excellent.*

Our wider circle of friends, including those with little or no experience with Down syndrome kids, also embraced Richard. My neighbor Karyne was one of them, and this was her recollection of getting to know Rich:

> I first met Richard in 2004 when his mum and stepdad moved to Wollombi to live. He must have been thirteen at the time. Only having just met his mother and not knowing her very well at all, I had no idea that her son had Down syndrome. When she introduced him to us, it occurred to me that as an adult I had actually never been introduced to someone with the syndrome before, which is rather odd when you think about it. I had no idea how the syndrome affects its host apart from knowing that muscle weakness can be an issue. I didn't know the extent of cognitive function, either, so I initially felt a little restrained in his presence. Richard was warm and engaging straightaway. It was very easy to have a conversation with him; the only stumbling block was when he talked a little fast, which made it harder for me to understand, but he simply repeated himself and then I got it.

Once we were settled into village life, the next task was deciding on a high school for Richard that would meet all his needs. Finding the right high school wasn't easy. Graeme and I had looked at many options, and although we were now in different relationships and both content in our separate lives, we always made sure that Richard knew he had both parents on his side. The decision came in a simple statement Richard made one morning:

"I want to go to St. Edmund's, because I don't want to come last anymore."

I was surprised by this comment; I never expected it, and also felt a deep pain of sadness for my son. Although he smiled his way through most of primary school, he no doubt started seeing his difference, his otherness. The kids in his class were lovely, but they had their own stuff; and although in their younger years they had helped, cajoled, and celebrated him, as they got older they left him behind. He was set different schoolwork, he didn't succeed in sport, and stuff just became harder. He had always been a terrific reader—another one that God had given me—and he comprehended most things. But there was just that learning, that comprehension on an academic level, that just didn't kick in. For my part, denial played a major role. I couldn't bear seeing him hurt because he didn't succeed the way his classmates did. We (his dad, his family, and I) applauded the smallest success, talking him up big-time. But it wasn't the same as being applauded by his peers at school.

St. Edmund's College catered to students with mild to moderate disabilities. Although it was ostensibly a Catholic school, it took in students from all faiths, and there was really only one prerequisite for attending: they did not take kids with difficult, violent behavioral issues. A small school of maybe sixty teenagers when we enrolled, it had just the right balance of academic learning, sport, fun, and the greatest gift of all: opportunities for an active social life. It had originally been a school for visually impaired students, but changed its focus when it saw a need for adolescents with intellectual disabilities.

We realized that we had to listen to our son. He knew instinctively what was best for him. I had to let go of my dream of him attending a regular school. I had wanted Richard to experience a big school campus. His dad had gone to a private school, and I wanted him to go to the canteen, run riot in the hallways, and cheer on the school football team. Big high schools offer opportunity and exposure. But this was not what our son wanted. Richard would be safe, happy, and well looked after at St. Edmund's. There would be no bullying or awkward situations. He would shine and stand out for the best reasons. He wanted this.

And I wanted what he wanted. Even so, yet again I found myself at odds when faced with other parents in Disability World and the relentless spirit of competition that went along with the constant fear and insecurities we all feel for our kids.

One day I ran into a friend at a shopping center; she was from Disability World. She asked what we had decided on for high school.

"Was it St. Leo's," she asked, "or I think you said you put his name down at Knox?"

Both schools are nongovernment, fee-paying, high-achieving, mainstream institutions. I could feel the lump in my throat as I realized what I had done. I had set the bar too high with my usual boastful ambition, and now I was going to have to either admit defeat (as that was where the conversation was headed) or add on a new line of defense.

"Ah, no," I replied. "We decided that St. Edmund's would be a better fit, and Richard really wants to go there."

"Oh, gee, I thought he was doing so well that he would naturally go to a mainstream school." She didn't try to hide the smugness in her voice. Her own son was about to go to "normal" school.

"Well, we felt that his friendship group was getting smaller, and he would be lost in a big high school," I said.

"Oh, that's a shame," she said.

She turned on her heel, leaving me doubting whether I had done the right thing by sending him to St. Edmund's. To this day I still justify that decision by telling people he needed his friends and that it was a small school with plenty of opportunities. At the same time, I try hard to remember that Richard's school placement, especially at that stage of his life, couldn't be about me or my desire to win the disability race. I was happy to see him make these big life decisions. As it turned out, he was quite good at it.

The principal of St. Edmund's, Brother Cyril, was a lovely man who truly wore his heart on his sleeve; you could see that he desperately wanted the students to have a good, stress-free school life. He was so connected to the students, and his faith seemed boundless—unlike mine at times. Excited, though perhaps a little cautious, Richard took in his first day at school with his usual joie de vivre mixed with a hint of shyness. As much as I liked to think of him as a teenager, in many ways he was still a little boy, small and gentle. Delighted to see some kids he knew, he quickly connected with both old and new friends. Looking around, realizing that this would be home for the next six years, made me feel calm, the calmest I had been in a very long time.

Still, there were issues. I couldn't get the measure of some of the students, and my internal debate was still raging over whether we had done the right thing as far as enrolling him there. Who were these teachers? Did they have the students' best interests at heart? So many questions. Would the staff look after him? Would he be safe? Would he relate to other kids with intellectual disabilities?

But by the end of the term, my questions were answered. It was going well. Richard was settled, happy, and pleased to be going to school. The next chapter had begun.

꙳

From the start, Richard was in the care of some excellent teachers. There was a lot more protocol than there had been at Mount Kuring-gai, our beloved mainstream primary school. At St. Edmund's you could enter the school only via security doors, as some kids liked to go wander off. Because of the varying medical issues of the students, there was already a lot of stuff in place to keep the kids safe and on the right track: no slacking off on school uniforms; frequent parent-teacher meetings that set the term goals . . . There was no slacking off on academics. The students were expected to learn. Classes were not about watching TV and coloring but true learning with books and Bunsen burners, school excursions, concerts, and award presentations. Richard enjoyed the smallness of the school, navigating his way around new rules, participating in debates, and making new friends. Some students troubled him. I knew they would. Aggressive, loud behavior always worried Richard. It was not so much that he was scared. Rather, he was overwhelmingly empathetic. He hated to see anyone distressed and didn't cope well with it. Tears came all too easily.

My goal was to get settled into our new environment before introducing even more new elements to our lives, including people. So I decided to hold off on playdates and sleepovers with any new classmates, which in our case would actually be more like weekend trips. More importantly, I didn't want to do that thing that many parents mistakenly do and invite kids over because they like the parents. The kids might not like each other at all. There was also a more pressing issue for me that I had to come to terms with: my own prejudice. When Richard was in primary school, I didn't have to worry about "disability" in the larger sense. But here in high school was a school full of kids with a wide range of disability. Down syndrome I could deal with. As for the rest, I was not so sure.

During that first year at St. Edmund's we all found our way around the system, made new friends, and got to know the teachers and the office staff. Rich struggled with some of the academic stuff. I think that was partly to do with the last year at Mount Kuring-gai, when funding had been harder to come by and he did not get that vital one-on-one education. At St. Edmund's we were lucky enough to have Judy Welsh as Richard's homeroom teacher for the first two years.

As Richard got older and more comfortable with his school surroundings, he started to enjoy learning. I loved listening to him describe all the things he was doing at school. Graeme was fabulous at making models with Richard, from volcanoes to train sets to woodworking projects. I loved that Richard could make things. I loved that he was actively participating in school life. I loved that he was not coming last anymore. I loved that he made me a pencil case for Christmas. There was some normality in that.

As soon as I started to chill out and let that appreciation kick in, everything became easier. Graeme was amazing at not stressing. In fact, I often questioned his relaxed attitude. But there was a method: Encourage what he is good at, don't freak out about the rest. Some things he just couldn't do. By far the most valuable gift Graeme gave to Richard was time, precious time. It helped Richard in so many immeasurable ways.

I began to love that I was not the only mum at the school who had a child with an intellectual disability: we all did. Woo-hoo! This village understood me and my son. In this village, there were still the same issues as parents with "normal" kids: you don't get on with some parents, there is always one kid who's a total pain in the arse or a teacher who really shouldn't be there; and all the other stuff that happens in school life. But at least with this village I didn't have to pretend or disguise anything. I had come a long way from my own prejudices, my own confusion about where I stood in Disability World. I did, however, miss being part of the old village and I had to accept that we had moved on.

Richard loved this village too. He was in a class of really fun kids. They were their own information service, social secretaries, and gossipers. They were tight. I loved them and all their funny little ways. I would just be getting to the canteen when one of them would advise me that Richard had accomplished something or that someone else had. They were the first to celebrate achievements and the last ones to complain. I loved them all for being Richard's friends, and I know he loved them too.

His greatest love, however, was performing. It was a fellow student and friend on the St. Edmund's school bus who introduced Richard to the stage, and he never looked back. Well, I should say she bossed him into performing, and I will always be thankful that she did. She encouraged him to join the St. Edmund's singing and dancing group. He was hooked. He loved moving those hips, singing those songs with the catchy lyrics, and practicing his moves. He soon became a permanent member of the school dance troupe—they became known as Eddie's Entertainers—and for the next six years he drove us all crazy with the constant repetition of whatever the next big concert was going to be. We went through it all: ABBA, the Beatles, Australian number ones. It was as exhausting as it was amazing.

These productions were mega. The school held them in conjunction with Abbotsleigh, a young women's private college not far from

St. Edmund's. It was part of their social justice program, and students would volunteer to help with the production, script, and choreography, and ensure that the St. Edmund's students had the maximum amount of fun. They started out as modest, cute, homegrown performances, but by the time Richard left St. Edmund's there was a cast of thousands on the stage with Richard singing his heart out and usually in the front row. Richard loved it and rejoiced in it. He practiced day in and day out, and when he wasn't practicing, he was calculating how many more sleeps before the big night.

Margriet Shaw-Taylor was the St. Edmund's teacher who put all this together. Her endless energy, passion, and sense of fun for the students were contagious. The auditorium was always full of parents, siblings, students, and teaching staff from both St. Edmund's and Abbotsleigh. Graeme was the official videographer and still is to this day. Every year he makes DVD copies for all the families, and Richard distributes them.

The sense of joy in the auditorium was unmistakable, and it gave Richard a real sense of purpose from year to year. For someone who was quite shy, he came alive on the stage. I enjoyed that part of Richard's personality, and St. Edmund's certainly encouraged his ability to perform, not just in song and dance, but whenever he was called upon to do important tasks for the school.

Judy Welsh recalls a big night in Richard's life:

One of the highlights of Richard's journey was reading the Grace in front of hundreds of people at one of the college's charity balls. Before the big event we spent some time practicing on his clarity of speech. On the night, he was very proud reading with confidence like a veteran. The smile on Richard's face is one I will always remember and treasure.

In 2007 it was time for Richard to learn how to catch public transport on his own. He was sixteen and it was the grown-up thing to do, or so he would tell us every other minute of every day until we gave the okay. A ten-minute walk to the train station, catching a train and riding it for six stops, getting off the train, crossing various roads, and then a fifteen-minute walk to the school. *Nope,* I thought, *he can't do that. I don't want him to do that. That's far too risky and dangerous. Not gonna happen.* But Richard wanted it to happen.

"I'm not a baby Mum," he said.

So he watched, learned, and listened, and before I knew it, there he was, independently getting himself to school. To make his mother feel better, as I was still living in Wollombi, he would call me when he was walking to the station and home again. Again, that question of independence can be a vexing one for parents of intellectually disabled children; they have their own set of family rules and family expectations. Some don't want their kids taking public transportation or going to the movies with their mates. That's up to them. Graeme and I both wanted Richard to have a full and meaningful life with every opportunity other teenagers had. We wanted him to experience the joys of independence and freedom. And, boy, did he walk tall.

The last two years of Richard's high school life showed significant changes in him. He embraced being a senior and the responsibilities that came with it. He took on a role of looking after younger students, was voted deputy school captain, and with that came attending more functions as a senior student. To watch not just Richard but his entire graduating class learn, participate, challenge, and question was so rewarding on many levels.

Can mainstream high schools offer that same cohesion and acceptance? I don't know, as I have never experienced that environment; but I have had friends who have, and they seemed happy with their child's education. I was more worried about the social aspect of Richard's life. There is also little in the way of research to back up evidence about special education versus mainstream, which is a pity, as we can never really tell how beneficial mainstream education is. What I have found interesting is that I have very rarely, maybe never, seen a quote from or heard a child with an intellectual disability tell it from their perspective. Yes, they may do better in math and other academic work, but how is their "lonely scale"? How do they rate their own inclusion in the playground? Parents often speak for their kids, saying it's great they are in mainstream, but are those kids socially happy? My bet would be they are not. In an article for the *Conversation*, academics Christopher Boyle, Jo Anderson, and Natalie Swayn state that

> there is no single nationally accepted definition of inclusive education or set of standards that have been established to describe what inclusive education is. Consequently, it means different things across different systems, and between different schools. Second, the tracking of academic progress of students with disabilities, especially those with intellectual or communication disabilities, is done poorly in Australia. Many of these students are on individual plans, which look different between systems, sectors and even schools.

I think back to what it was like for me as a kid going to school. Did any of my schoolmates have an intellectual disability? Probably, but they weren't labeled; we just thought they were annoying and badly behaved. The dressmaker's daughter, Pauline, went to a special school for her entire school life. There were certainly no inclusion policies or special classes in mainstream school.

I saw students at St. Edmund's who had successfully attended mainstream primary schools, then went to a mainstream high school, but who moved to St. Edmund's in year eight (age thirteen) because they'd become socially isolated at school. My friend Tracylee told me of a young man with Down syndrome who was the only person with an intellectual disability in his year at school. He spent the last three years of schooling eating recess and lunch outside the principal's office because he didn't "belong" anywhere. How can that happen?

St. Edmund's was not always smooth sailing. There were times when I questioned some decisions that the teaching staff made; even the most dedicated teacher can sometimes not push kids hard enough because of their disabilities. Again, I was striving for the best. We did not always see eye to eye, but at least the door was always open. The impact of the social life that St. Edmund's offered is still evident. All these years later, we still have a close circle of friends from our time there.

I asked Richard to write about his experience at St. Edmund's:

### St. Edmund's by Richard

2004: I started at St. Edmund's, I was nervous because it was a new school. It was a nice school, I had some friends there as well. Their names—Jess, Madeline and Alex. My fist teacher was Mrs. Welsh and Jeanie. My first concert was *Joseph*, I liked doing it.

2005: I moved in to Year 8. In that was Kevin, Ben, Aaron, Katherine, Crystal, Elizabeth and some other kids. Mrs. Welsh was still my teacher; Mrs. Laing started as the receptionist. My second concert was ABBA. I loved ABBA.

2006: I moved in to Year 9. Mrs. Shaw-Taylor was my teacher, that was Jim's last year at school. I learned food tech and travel training. I liked travel training because I was becoming independent. The next one of our performances was the Beatles.

2007: I moved in to Year 10. I sat for my school certificate. My subjects were creative arts, PE, maths, religion, English. That was Ashley's last year. My next one was Aussie Greats. My teacher was Margriet. I caught the train on my own.

2008: I moved into Year 11. I did TAFE, I did business and work experience at Phil McCarrolls Toyota. I did office work [at]

Raine and Horne. I liked it a lot. My next concert was *Eddie's High School Musical*—that was lot fun.

2009: This my last year of school. I was the school vice captain. I was good at it. I had a formal. My last concert was *World Tour*. I went to a school retreat near Penrith.

$\star$

School was going well, and Wollombi, with its rich history and interesting inhabitants—both human and nonhuman—continued to weave its magic on us. My partner took to the garden and would often get a very reluctant Richard to come outdoors to help him. Rich was initially timid around him, finding his big and often difficult personality hard to manage. My partner did not appear to really understand or see Richard's disability, so there was often conflict about how to manage their relationship.

It was complicated. We had many big dinner parties where Richard would happily spend part of the night talking with adults and helping with the dishes, all the stuff kids do, and then boredom would set in, which usually meant Richard would want to head downstairs to watch TV. Rich was addicted to TV. He would watch repeat episodes of all his favorite shows: *The Simpsons*, *Mother and Son*, and *WWF Superstars of Wrestling*. Then it was either watching sports on TV or playing with his PlayStation. He was happiest in front of the box, especially when the only other option was a boring dinner party with adults, but my partner wanted him to be present, to socialize and enjoy what we were enjoying. He expected that from both the boys, but they were boys. It's a great thing to want, but it wasn't necessarily what Richard wanted. It was, at times, a real battle.

The TV was on from the moment Rich woke up. It never bothered me, as I always thought it was a great way for him to build his language skills. Even as a toddler I had him sitting watching *Barney* (that crazy purple dinosaur), *Play School*, and *Sesame Street*. He enjoyed the shows and I enjoyed the time. I know that sounds like a cop-out, but I had observed my Maltese mother's English improve after years of watching *The Young and the Restless, Days of Our Lives,* and her all-time favorite, *The Bold and the Beautiful.* Not only did her English improve, but so did her confidence and her wardrobe.

For Richard, TV also seemed to be a source of calm, so I was more than okay with his addiction. But my partner was not, and—as men often do—he wanted Richard busy outdoors. He valued getting your hands dirty, breathing in fresh air, and because he had grown up in the English countryside, he felt it was vital for good health and well-being to spend more time outdoors than in. I totally understood this, as I love it too. But for Richard the outdoors, with its snakes and creepy crawlies, was a scary place. He did not have the balance needed to do some of the more challenging outdoor stuff, like carrying wood, using a wheelbarrow, or climbing steep hills. They eventually compromised. My partner would make sure tasks were minimized to ensure success. I was glad they did, as I think it helped them appreciate the other.

Although there were issues like this, there was still love and respect. A mother and child can sometimes see things very differently. Richard was once asked by a career counselor who he most valued in his life. Of course, it was the usual round of his mum, dad, grandma, and family. But then he said this: "I really like my stepdad, as he is the only one that speaks to me like an adult." It was an instructive moment in my life. Respect, above so much else, was truly important to Richard. Thereafter, I took my cue on how Richard saw himself from that one revealing comment.

↘

My own relationship with my partner was complicated. We worked in our business together, but he was also consulting and was away a great deal. It was often only during weekends that we saw each other, and that was when Richard was visiting. My stepson, meanwhile, was still in New Zealand. We were a family of four, constantly separated, each desperately hoping for the undivided attention of the other. Even as I write, I am conflicted about how to fairly describe our dynamic.

The boys were fine with each other. Although only a few years apart, they could not have been more different, but my stepson showed great maturity in how he accepted Richard. He became his advocate in a way; often he thought I was too harsh on Rich and would defend him. Richard, meanwhile, instinctively knew that his stepbrother needed time with his dad when he was with us for the holidays.

The two of them, and the two puppies, which had grown into very large dogs, hung out together. It was natural, and they had each other's backs. Over a long summer holiday and with the greatest of skill, Richard's stepbrother taught him how to swim. This came after a life-time fear of water. Richard had always wanted to swim but refused to ever put his head underwater—that is, until his stepbrother patiently guided him through the motions. Sitting on the deck, I'd listen to their conversation from the pool: "This is what you do, this is how you do it, and I am here to help you manage it."

My stepson was caring and nurturing, a natural teacher, and be-fore I knew it, Richard was swimming. Then there were the races, some of which Richard "won." My stepson was an excellent swimmer. He was a fish. In time, Richard became one too.

Stepfamilies are not easy to be in at times. It takes a world of un-derstanding to make them work as effectively and seamlessly as might be possible. In many respects, I think my partner and I tried to the best of our abilities, but on many levels we failed—as our marriage eventually did. I heard this quote once and am not entirely sure where it comes from: "You carry in your soul every ingredient necessary to turn your existences into joy; all you have to do is mix those ingredi-ents." I think our individual recipes took precedence over the family meal. It was never the banquet I wanted it to be.

Richard was not oblivious to the undercurrent of difficulties in the marriage. He would comment on certain behaviors and at times on my loneliness whenever my partner was away. What Richard enjoyed at these times was having his mother to himself. He-and-me time was becoming a blessing for us both.

Richard loved getting to know people and being in the hub of village life. As usual he ended up knowing more people than I did, but that's so Richard. Sally and Steve, who owned the general store, put him front and center with customers; Bruno at the local café had him serving customers; and Caroline, who ran a bed-and-breakfast, had him helping her in the kitchen. They were all great life experiences and great life relationships. It doesn't take much to make a person with an intellectual disability part of a workplace or a community. The more I reflect on the opportunities Richard had in Wollombi, the more I have come to understand that what's important is the open-heartedness and patience of people willing to have a go, to take a risk, to show guidance and not take it all so seriously.

Richard's friends from school now started to come for weekend visits. As would have been the case with any group of teenage boys, the downstairs level became a den of iniquity—not quite in the biblical sense, but it certainly had all the trappings. There were piles of food, half-finished drinks, dishevelment, and odors. There was much laughter, banter, teasing, and competition. The pool was used regularly. My biggest fear was always their inability to react quickly enough to any danger, especially the wriggly kind. I had not ever imagined that I would be the one to put them in real danger.

It happened one Saturday afternoon when my partner was having a siesta. Our bedroom was upstairs, where a wraparound veranda hugged the outside of the house. It looked down on the garden and the pool. I was in the kitchen, when I heard my partner calling my name in a somewhat distressed state.

"Benny! Benny! Get a broom—get something! There is a snake in here!"

Firstly, he is English, and so he didn't grow up in the wild place that is the Australian bush. Second, he seemed never to close a door, which I'd warned him about when we moved to the country. I walked in, broom at the ready, only to be greeted by a petrified, six-foot-six bloke standing on the bed. Guess I couldn't blame him. Those things can kill you.

"It's over there."

"Where?"

"Behind the curtain."

And there it was, the tiniest of red-bellied black snakes. I was a bit stupid to assume it was docile because it was small, but I started to sweep it out of the room and out onto the deck, sending it flying over the edge. Then it hit me: Richard and his friend were in the pool below. Red-bellied black snakes like to swim. I raced downstairs, my mind spinning. How would I explain to the boy's parents that I had flung a snake onto their unsuspecting son? Fortunately, they were oblivious to any danger, and the little snake disappeared into the bushes.

We held birthday parties, end-of-year parties, and all sorts of parties for Richard and his friends at that house. I loved that he had such great social skills and clearly enjoyed how we entertained. My partner and I enjoyed the good things in life: we laid on far too much in the way of food and drink but loved doing it. Whenever we went shopping, Richard's conversation would be all about whether we had enough food, or he'd remind me that someone only drank a certain brand of soft drink. Then he'd decide a cheese platter would be nice and again express concern that we may not have enough snacks.

We spent wonderful years in Wollombi, and it was devastating for us to move on when the time came. When I told Richard that his stepdad and I were splitting up, he was quite philosophical about it. It was clear he'd expected this and that he was acutely aware of the faults in the marriage. Loss and grief come to us for many reasons and present in many ways. I was feeling pretty low about it all, but my son encouraged me to look at life with a cup half-full.

My partner moved back to New Zealand and I was left with the daunting task of selling the property and all that went with that. When you live on one hundred acres, there are all sorts of things like chain saws, rotary hoes, and lawn tractors that you really don't need in suburbia. Suburbia! How could I move to suburbia after thirteen years on the land? The thought of this totally freaked me out. I could move a lot closer to Richard, but all I could afford was an apartment, and with the two dogs that seemed a little problematic, to say the least. They had only ever known Wollombi, so I had to consider them, myself, and Richard.

Water had always been important to me—and to Richard. Many of our holidays were spent frolicking around the ocean, so I made the decision to go coastal. I wanted to be able to visit Richard more regularly, and I also wanted him to be able to get to me. Now that he was older and no longer at school, I wanted him to be able to make choices about when he wanted to see me, when we could just hang out or arrange at short notice to go to a movie or lunch.

I found my new place, a tiny home, but it would be the place where I could breathe, reflect, and grow. It would be my new beginning.

# 7

# Ya Gotta Have Friends

"Each friend represents a world in us, a world
not born until they arrive, and it is only by
this meeting that a new world is born."
—ANAÏS NIN

Friendship is a gift with the power to magnify the beauty and joy of living. While it can also be a source of heart-crushing disappointment, most of my friendships have enriched and challenged me. Being the social creature that I am, I was always hyperaware of Richard's social interactions. I didn't want Richard to be an only child with no friends, with a disability, and with sadness and pity surrounding him. He deserved better than that.

While he had certainly made friends at Mount Kuring-gai, the significant differences between him and the rest of the student body became more and more evident as they all got older. As a result, it became more of a challenge to maintain the friendships he'd made when he was younger. Now that they were teenagers, conversations and playtime no longer came as easily as they had before.

At St. Edmund's I had assumed—stupidly, as it turns out—that Richard would be drawn to students who were more like him: kids with Down syndrome. But it wasn't like that at all. When Richard hit St. Edmund's, a whole new social life opened up for him. From the moment we walked into that school, Richard had new friends, girls and boys with various disabilities, in all shapes and sizes.

Graeme and I had always been on the same page when it came to issues involving disability. It was not going to dominate our entire world, which meant it would certainly not define Richard's. Going to St. Edmund's meant we had to revise that philosophy, however. Looking back, it almost seems that Richard might have chosen St. Edmund's not just for his sake but for ours too. It gave Graeme and me the gentle reality check we would need to prepare Richard for adult life and to prepare ourselves for the years ahead. But, best of all, it gave Richard a bounty of lifelong friends.

His year seven class, the commencing high school class, was a mixture of many diversities. Our Disability World had mostly consisted of Down syndrome, but in this new place there were kids there with all sorts of autism, all sorts of learning disorders, all sorts of genetic makeups. There were also white kids, black kids, Middle Eastern kids, and Asian kids. Some had different gods and all came from various socioeconomic backgrounds. Some came from the surrounding suburbs and some from miles away. Buses provided transport for those who came long distances.

We were delighted to see some of the other kids we had known from our early days at Macquarie. Not only did we like the kids, but we liked their families. They were a part of our Down syndrome village, and in that there was some sense of safety and camaraderie. It also meant that I knew what I was dealing with. I really wanted to encourage those friendships. But what is that old saying: "When we plan, God laughs"? One thing I had missed out on when I was traveling and living abroad was that Richard was no longer a pliable kid, willing to go along with whatever Mum thought was best. He was now a teenager who wanted to make his own decisions about who he spent his time with.

Enter Michael Karseboom.

It wasn't just God laughing. It was all of us—joyfully.

Michael and Richard. What a pair. Complete and total opposites.

Michael was a string bean, all arms and legs, and to make it even more interesting, he was South African and Jewish. Michael had been born perfectly healthy. However, as a little baby he kept dying, and every time he was resuscitated, the oxygen to his brain became depleted. Consequently, Michael had mild cerebral palsy, intellectual disability, and dyspraxia. But he was blessed with a mother who worked her butt off to get him moving. Anthea made it her mission to ensure her son's disability would not get in the way of him having the best life he could. Now he never stops.

Michael and Richard developed a beautiful friendship right away, one that was built around fun, chatter, laughter, and a healthy dose of competition. They brought out the best in each other. Michael's passion for activity meant Rich had to get off his arse and move. Richard's passion for watching TV and playing PlayStation meant Michael had to sit on his butt and just be. I loved listening to their conversations. The bond they were developing was important to them both. They learned how to negotiate, compromise, assess, and analyze how they would be in a friendship situation.

Since Richard was an only child, some of those skills didn't come easily to him. Michael had an older sibling, loving and kind, but she was female. These two very "boy" boys started to work out how to be in a teenage male friendship. It was a defining friendship for Richard. As well as having a great time together, they also fought and got cranky and sullen with each other, but those moments were the exception and not the rule. Nothing made me happier than hearing them laugh and curse.

As Michael put it, "What I liked about my friendship with Richard was the fact that I could talk to him about anything and he was never mean. Very caring boy. Over the years some good memories that stand out for me are going to Wollombi and going to schoolies after year twelve and having lots of holidays together and boys' nights, sleepovers, going to the club and dancing to ABBA. First beer together in Port Macquarie."

Richard was incredibly loyal and caring in this friendship, as was Michael. Rich always told me what Michael could or could not eat.

"Mum, don't forget, you can't put ham on the pizza, because Mike can't eat it."

"Yes. I know, Rich."

"He can't eat prawns, either, Mum."

"Yes. I know that, too, Richard."

"And you have to—"

"Yes! I know, Richard!"

"Just reminding you because remember you forgot last week."

Smarty-pants. He never forgets anything.

Through Michael, Richard experienced the Jewish way of life. Michael's mum, Anthea, included Richard in their religious traditions. Richard loved these extra holidays and occasions, so much so that I am pretty sure he would have liked to adopt both faiths, so as to double the cause for celebration in his life.

Michael often came along on holidays with me, Richard, and my mum and dad. My parents loved him and loved having both the boys to themselves. Most summers, we would rent a place by the sea for a week and enjoy relaxing throughout the day. With the setting of the sun, the fellowship and joy of being in each other's company would take a serious turn. After dinner, with everyone seated at the table, drinks in hand, silence prevailed. It was time for the Uno cards to come out. Eyes would widen, all directed at the dealer. The game was on: no largesse, no acts of kindness. Every man for himself amid screams of laughter, accusations of cheating, sometimes tears, and more laughter. Before we knew it, it would be midnight. My father often headed off to bed with a cheeky grin, knowing he had scammed the boys again: he'd hide cards under his seat. They were often found by Michael. Grandpa again! They'd chase him down the hallway; he would plead his innocence. Richard loved this time, and so did I.

Many years later, when Richard was being interviewed for a possible work placement, he was asked a few questions by the head of the department.

"Richard, I see here that you have noted that you are Catholic, so I am assuming that you will want all the holidays of Easter and Christmas to spend with your family?"

"Yes, thank you."

"Are there any other holidays or special days you would like to have away from work?" she asked innocently.

"Yes, please, I would like to have Hanukkah, please."

I laughed and laughed, but she didn't get the joke, so Richard explained.

"My best friend, Michael, is Jewish and it's a good holiday, so I want it off too."

One thing that I had not anticipated was Richard's magnetism. He was cute but in many ways shy. He eventually had a lot of friends and sometimes, I thought, far too many. But each friendship delivered something new. It made Richard think about how to navigate other people's needs and not be entirely focused on his own.

In his homeroom class Richard often took it upon himself to help those he felt were struggling. His empathy and desire to help became a priority for him. He would often burst into tears, saying something like "I'm really worried about Tom. He was really upset at school today."

Richard crying is a pretty gruesome affair. He wails and blubbers and can't quite compose himself. Usually alarmed at the ferocity of the outburst, I would try to console him, but sometimes all I could do was laugh at the disproportionate intensity of his emotions. There is no evidence to say that people with Down syndrome cry more often or more intensely than their non–Down syndrome peers, but for Richard this was, maybe, just a way of expressing his grief. Although he has a lot of words, perhaps at times he just can't find the right ones. At times the event was nothing as big as what he made it out to be.

"Why was Hamish so upset, honey?" I might inquire.

"He forgot to bring his lunch with him today."

"Oh, for God's sake, Richard, it's hardly the end of the world."

He also had trouble with social conventions, and at times I became very exasperated.

We would be out shopping and if I was friendly to a shop assistant this type of exchange would happen.

"Who's she, Mum?" he asked, indicating a woman at the store (or school, doctor's office, whatever).

"She just works here."

"Do you know her?"

"No, I am just making conversation. It's what people do."

"But you told her about your weekend."

"Well, yes. She asked if I was doing anything interesting."

"So you know her."

"No, I don't know her!"

And on it would go, on and on, until I finally lost it and told him to shut up.

There are two schools of thought regarding how kids with Down syndrome pick up on social cues and expectations naturally. Academics Sue Buckley, Gillian Bird, and Ben Sacks say that because the children are strong visual learners, they "have the ability to learn daily social routines by imitating or copying others. Learning by imitation is a strength for children with Down syndrome, and they pick up information about social behavior by watching others (both in real life and from drama activities or television shows)." The other, from research by Kari-Anne Næss, Egil Nygaard, Johanne Ostad, Anne-Stine Dolva, and Solveig-Alma Halaas Lyster, says that children with Down syndrome have, in general, weaker social capabilities compared with other kids of a similar mental age. Either point of view can be partially supported by the evidence; however, a constant theme through both is that delayed language development in kids with Down syndrome affects their ability to relate to others socially. This could also be compounded by hearing impairment and vision impairment, both of which are common in children with Down syndrome.

Richard didn't seem to have any issues with social engagement other than wanting too much of it. Be careful what you wish for. I wanted Richard to understand that talking to people, having good manners, listening, and engaging would endear him to others. It was probably more my need to be accepted as a mother of a child with Down syndrome as well, but I also wanted people to see Richard, not just see a person with a disability. He'd observe me and his dad and others, and how we talked to people. To his credit, he learned. He learned how to strike up conversations, however disarming they could sometimes be. He was so good at it that some of my friends would put this skill to use. A lovely male friend was over from New Zealand, and Richard and I took him shopping for groceries. I was busy getting stuff, when Richard and our friend walked a little ahead of me and our friend spotted a beautiful woman at the checkout queue. He motioned ten-year-old Richard forward and they stood behind this woman in the queue. I could see he was loading Rich up with chocolates, and as I approached the checkout he said to Rich, "Say hi and ask her what her name is." So Rich promptly tapped this woman on the back and said, "Hi, my name is Richard. What's yours?"

"Hi, Richard," she replied. "My name is Natalie."

"Hi, Natalie. This is my friend and he would like your phone number."

I was furious and told my friend so. He never got the phone number, but Richard got the chocolates. That was Richard's modus operandi. "Hi, my name is Richard. What's yours? This is my mum, she needs a boyfriend, and she is thirty-seven." He seriously did this to me after his dad and I split up. I could have killed him.

Situations like this often confused me. I became quite conflicted. Do I publicly admonish Rich, knowing that doing so might hurt his feelings? If I don't—if I pretend nothing enormously awkward has occurred—will that just make the situation harder? Will it add to the perception that people with Down syndrome don't have the capacity to engage, converse, and communicate? In Richard's case, he always knew what he wanted to say; he just sometimes couldn't say it and would trip over his words. I had to learn to be quiet at times. He had to learn to speak for himself.

I tried hard not to finish his sentences or repeat more clearly what he'd said when we were out in public. It was also about accepting that his disability would never change and that it had to be me who adjusted and adapted. There was no quick fix guide, nor was there any real formal training for parenting a child with Down syndrome. There was a plethora of academic jargon regarding Down syndrome that I sometimes got my head around, and we were lucky that Robin and Sue at Macquarie University gave us some great tips regarding some known behaviors. But the reality is that, like any parenting, you just have to use your intuition. I remember Dr. Grass, Richard's pediatrician, saying these words to me: "No one will know Richard better than you and his dad. Trust yourself." It took me a long time to do that, and a long time to adjust and accept. I had to let go of my fears and shame and just go with his way of seeing the world. But I also had to ensure that although at times what he said and asked was inappropriate and disarming, it was never allowed to be rude or uncaring. What I didn't want was for Richard to be seen as the disabled kid who was rude.

I am not entirely sure how I managed this, but through all the chaos of learning, adapting, and questioning, I made the time to explain to Richard why things work the way they work, why relationships are built and nurtured. Arduous as it sometimes was, the reward has been that Richard can now hold his own with just about anyone. He is social and engaging, and at times inappropriate.

Although socializing with the outside world was still a work in progress, the friendship group from St. Edmund's multiplied. They were a tight, cliquey group, with their leaders, followers, and joiners. There were also the gossips, the troublemakers, and the jealous ones, just as in any other high school cohort. They were nothing less than teenagers doing what teenagers do. Richard both reveled and rejoiced in this gang. He had his favorites, but he also had those who he was quite happy to keep at a distance.

It took me a while to work out that Richard's lovely, compliant nature was starting to change a little. He was becoming more aware of personalities and how others behaved. If he found someone challenging, he would give them a wide berth. If he didn't particularly like someone, he would not really engage with them. At times it was confusing for him. The nuances of relationships are difficult at the best of times when communication is not clear, and Richard sometimes found his school mates confronting. Richard had to adjust in many ways. He could no longer rely on his cuteness and difference as being a means to getting his own way, which he did often both at his primary school and with his family. He had to learn that Mum and Dad were not going to be there to hold his hand and fight his battles. He had to do that on his own.

As pleased as I was that he had found new friends who understood him, I felt very strongly that I wanted him to have as many relationships as possible outside of Disability World. Since he was an only child, I didn't want that to be his only behavior marker, especially as he was transitioning from boy to man. I wanted him to be aware that what was appropriate for some might not be as appropriate for others.

Although his cousins and family were ever-present, encouraging, and loving, with that comes a wide range of acceptance, forgiveness, and "getting away with blue murder." Those family ties, as great as they were, were creating a kid who would too frequently get his own way, was totally spoiled, and was loved beyond scrutiny—meaning that if things went wrong, he would have a massive meltdown. My mother, the uber-cleaner from hell, would allow Richard to run his little fingerprints all over her newly polished windows. No one else got away with that. His aunties sometimes told him not to worry about what Mum said. They would always spoil him. He was absolutely aware of this, and he knew totally how to work the system. He couldn't complete his homework tasks because "I am so tired, Mum," but he could articulate to his auntie Lu that he was more than ready to go out for an ice cream.

What I wanted was to teach Rich some resilience and fortitude to ensure that his cuteness was not the only method of getting what he wanted or standing well in this world. I also knew that not everyone would think: *Cute kid with Down syndrome.* I didn't want the "sympathy" reward for him. I wanted people to appreciate Richard for Richard. My mission was to get him some friends outside the normal channels. Even at St. Edmund's, the other parents would say what a lovely kid he was, what nice manners he had, and what a beautiful smile. All that was, of course, true, but none of it challenged him or put him in a place that wasn't full of support. I was worried that he wasn't really out in the real world.

One day I was talking to the school secretary, Cathy. She is one of those people who will pick up straightaway if you walk into a room looking upset. There's no escaping her *Are you okay?* radar, and I love her for it. I was not in my usual crazy rush of running in and running out that morning, so for once I thought to ask Cathy if *she* was okay. She was not displaying her usual calm demeanor.

"Just worried about my son, Cam. He seems so rudderless."

We got to talking. As it turned out, Cam had recently graduated from high school and wasn't quite sure what he should be doing. He was a lovely young man, gentle and smart. I was looking to expand Richard's social network with some kids that did not have an intellectual disability. Bing: lightbulb moment.

"Do you think he would be interested in hanging out with Rich?"

So began an unlikely but truly great friendship. Rich and Cam hung out together, and Rich met Cam's friends, and they hung out too. What was apparent from the start was that Cam really didn't mind too much what I thought; it wasn't about me and my needs. He was only interested in what Rich thought and what Rich wanted to do. I was excited by this, but also a little petrified. So was Cathy, as she explained:

Cameron and Richard started to meet. Firstly, they went to the movies and had dinner. They met with Cameron's friends— which terrified me but thrilled Richie! Cam was never keen to go to the movies. He said it was a "waste of time with Richard"—two hours where you couldn't talk! They went fishing and played video games. I would come home to find them cooking in my kitchen and then disappearing downstairs to the abyss that was known as "the Mexican room." Hours would go by before Cam finally would drive Richard home. Cam was a six-foot-four-inch, long-haired, interesting character and I used to wonder at the ease both Benny and Graeme had in letting Richie go off with him in his car—but let him they did, and the two grew into quite a pair. Richie was well known and well loved by Cam's friends and just became one of the pack. Unfortunately, Cam's friends were well-known in the local area and not always for all the right reasons, but Richard's parents wanted a "different but normal" friendship. This they got!

I was also very happy to see Richard discovering new friends— and a new interest—through rugby league. When I began high school, I became very passionate about rugby league. It was a game that crossed all divides. Looking back to that time, I think that for immigrants like myself it was part of fitting in with the Australian way of life. My team, Parramatta, was my passion, and I got to many games and suffered the highs and (mostly) lows of supporting an often lack-luster team. That is until the year they won the Grand Final. I can still relive the euphoria and excitement. All I could talk about at the time was the win and my team, the champions.

Sport is a great leveler. Just about everyone has a team, and I wanted to encourage Richard to follow one, to understand the game, to be a part of a tribe of fans. He had picked up on my love for the game, and his dad liked rugby too. I assumed that Richard would at least support one of our teams, so I was totally devastated when he chose his uncle Graham's beloved St. George Illawarra Dragons. That he chose a team I actively disliked was galling in the extreme. And he knew it. With that look of innocence, he would say, "But you still love me, Mum."

His love for the Dragons didn't last too long. He found a new team, and a better team at that, when he switched to underdogs the South Sydney Rabbitohs and became a "Bunnies" supporter through and through. I signed him up to become a member and he has been devoted ever since. It's an obsession to this day. For six months of the year, all he talks about is rugby league. Here's why he likes the game:

> The best part of being a fan is that it's fun to watch. I love yelling at the referees because sometimes they are really dumb. I enjoy the biffos [slang for "fistfights"]. I like talking to people about the games. I like teasing my mates and especially my mother.
>
> At the Grand Final I like seeing the players that are retiring as we give them a good send-off. My favorite players are Greg Inglis, Adam Reynolds, and Sam Burgess. The Melbourne Storm is my second-best team (because I met them at work) and I really like Cameron Smith, Cameron Munster, and Will Chambers. Everyone was really nice to me that night. At the Grand Final when the Rabbitohs won I went off my head. It was really amazing. Soooo happy and I kept talking about it for a long time.

That Grand Final was, I think, the happiest day of his life, and he still talks about it. He has an amazing knowledge of the game: the players, the coaches, and all things league. He can discuss a game at great length and has no pause button when it comes to telling you how poorly your team has performed. But he is also a really good sport and stays positive even when his Bunnies go down.

At first, I would support the same team as Richard whenever we attended a Grand Final. I thought, naïvely, that he would want me to cheer for the same team. We'd be bonding. After about the third year he asked me which team I was following and promptly chose the other. My team was not going to win, he told me. And he was right. When we back opposing teams, he will simply say, "You're going down, Mum."

Strange things happen at football games, and even stranger ones at Grand Finals. I was still nervous with Richard and big crowds, as he was not great with his balance and stairs, and found a lot of noise difficult, which is not uncommon for young people with Down syndrome. I would buy good tickets so that we didn't have too many stairs to climb. Over the years my blood would boil whenever I rang to buy disabled-seating tickets with easy access to the exit, fewer stairs, and bathrooms nearby, only to be told they were sold out. Not only were the amenities nicer but the view was great. On the day of the game those seats were often occupied by people who clearly didn't need them. Sometimes, if I made enough noise, I would get those tickets, but I eventually realized that some battles are just too hard to win. I also felt I was encouraging the notion that Richard should be treated as disabled. I once accidentally parked in a disabled parking spot and realized it just as we were about to get out of the car. I explained to Richard where I'd parked.

"Well, you'd better move, Mum. I am not disabled," Richard said. I did what I was told.

Disability can be seen or not seen. What I have found at a football match is that Richard is not seen as disabled but as part of the tribe attending the match. It started with our first-ever Grand Final. We are always early but not as early as the group of men sitting in front of us on this day. They were clearly a group of mates there to enjoy the whole day. One by one, as they got up to head to the bar, they would pass Richard with a "G'day, mate" or a "Who ya goin' for, mate?" and a "Should be a good game, mate." As the day wore on and the relationship between Richard and the men cemented, the banter extended to rubbing the top of his head every time they went past with a "Good on ya, mate." One of them even offered Richard a beer. Richard was underage, but he was in their tribe.

"A beer wouldn't hurt, Mum."

They didn't see him for his disability but simply as a young man at the footy barracking for their team.

Over the years, we must have bought our Grand Final tickets at the same time, because we often found this group sitting near us. It was really great to have them close by and have this familiarity with them. I was still nervous about Richard being in big crowds, and their presence made it safer somehow. They were from Dubbo, a faraway rural town. Each year Richard would really look forward to seeing them and would clock them well before I did.

"Mum, the Dubbo men are here!"

Richard's passion for the game has given him an enormous amount of confidence over the years. For a ten-year-old kid who couldn't put two and two together, he quickly learned how many points it would take to win a match. Now, despite his speech at times being not so clear, he has no trouble pronouncing the most difficult names: Brad Takairangi, Sam Tagataese, Suaia Matagi, Jesse Sene-Lefao, and my particular favorite, Tepai Moeroa. Richard will fall over laughing at my pronunciation and enjoys correcting me far too much.

As attractive as winning is to Richard, he has an acceptance of defeat. He wears a game loss well most of the time, but there have been times when his relaxed temperament gives way to a fury that I very seldom see. It is all about the injustice he feels at bad decisions made by the referee, who is usually at the receiving end of his tirade. I have to stop myself from laughing; I just cannot believe this raging person is my sweet boy. It's scary; he really knows how to swear. (I can't imagine where he got it.) But he is the happiest person on Earth when the Bunnies win. There is nothing more joyful than Richard's smile on a win day.

This year his beloved South Sydney Rabbitohs are doing really well, and Richard is ecstatic. Each year members of our family and extended family are in an online tipping competition. Basically, each week you make a selection of winning teams in your own competition. Our competition is one of many. As a player you can view not only your standing in your immediate competition, but also your standing in the whole competition. It's great fun, and Richard takes it very seriously. This year he is killing it and coming first in our competition. We were looking at the results online the other day, when I noticed, for the first time, that you can actually see where you stand in the bigger picture of all the competitions and all the other players nationally. I could not believe what I was seeing: my son, my gorgeous boy, this kid was coming 123rd out of 99,870 players. Now, that's worth celebrating!

# 8

# Boy to Man

"No matter how long you train someone to be brave, you
never know if they are or not until something real happens."
—VERONICA ROTH

When the looming realization hit that Richard would soon be graduating from St. Edmund's, I surprised myself by not going into total panic mode. In a dream world, if Richard could have stayed at St. Edmund's forever, I would have been happy. But life isn't dream world, and although Richard was apprehensive, he wanted to get out there and try something new.

What do we do when we leave school? Get a job? Go to college? Take a gap year? Launch our own YouTube channel? Choices are limited if you have an intellectual disability. There were really only two options available to Richard then: he could either join a program called community participation, which offered a lot of arts and crafts, outings, recreational activities, and perhaps some volunteer work, or a program called Transition to Work (TTW).

Having had some work experience in Wollombi, Richard was keen to join the workforce. He wanted to be like any other young adult, out there earning a living. Locally there was very little in the way of a really good, robust TTW program. The ones that were offered didn't take the students or their abilities to engage in useful work seriously, and mostly offered piecemeal work; and although you could say the work would suit someone with a low IQ, it did not allow for a person's capacity to grow in that job. Stacking shelves, cleaning, and the like are all fine jobs, but was it the best job for that student? The funding also restricted what could be achieved by the service providers. I was appalled to learn that the TTW program covered only two days a week. The other three days were not their problem, so I assumed that meant it was all right for Richard to sit on his arse for three days. Well, that wasn't going to happen—not on my watch. It wasn't going to happen to any of Richard's friends, either.

Leaving high school is a transition for anyone. For Richard, it was no different. All of us wanted him to have a secure working future. A real job. Halfway through his final high school year, I became frustrated about our options, so I approached Deirdre Cheers, the executive officer of CatholicCare Diocese of Broken Bay. I had known Deirdre through my sister, Martha. Richard had already participated in a number of CatholicCare recreational activities—bowling, sporting events, various trips—and he had enjoyed them. They were well-planned, age-appropriate activities with committed staff. From there, I was introduced to the head of Disability Services, Trish Devlin. I explained to Trish what I wanted: a TTW program for our local area to service the kids coming out of St. Edmund's and anywhere else.

Trish and the team at CatholicCare looked at my proposal and they saw the need for a program, and before I knew it, we had lift-off. Trish gave me so much hope that this could work. And it did. Premises were secured, programs designed, and enrollments taken. I could hardly believe that someone had paid attention to a need in our community. I really felt that, not only were we on the threshold of achieving something great, but I was gaining strength in being more proactive in Richard's life.

Securing all that we did in such a short period of time, it was now D-day. Richard had finished at St. Edmund's in December, and it was now early January: TTW was open and the year commenced with an enrollment of twelve young people. Watching Richard walk into the premises that day was like watching him win an Academy Award. He walked tall and purposefully up those stairs. The next phase in his life was there, right in front of him, and he knew it. He had his own measure, and it was marvelous to watch. I was quite unprepared for my own feelings about this.

As much as I wanted this for Richard, in that crazy place that I hold inside to deposit my fears and worries, I still heard a tiny whisper of sadness calling out to me. Long gone were the dread and anxiety over my concerns for Richard, and my guilt over our separation. Long gone, too, was my need for him to be a genius and a star. I was in a good place with him and us. But perhaps that whisper of sadness came with the realization that he was now growing up. At eighteen he was no longer my little boy, the one I could expect to react in certain ways, the one I could mold into the person I wanted him to be. He had long been testing the boundaries with me, pushing "independence" buttons. No longer would he walk side by side with me at the shops. He would often choose to hang out in the game store while I did my shopping, or go and see a completely different movie from the one I wanted.

He will kill me for writing this, but the other big thing that happened was that he was becoming quite masculine. He was hairy, smelly, and blokey. Gone was his boyish physique. He was male—far too male in some respects, which both amused and concerned me. How would I mother a man? It was a strange place to be in, but I knew deep down that anxiety wasn't going to change anything or make me feel better, so I simply let it settle and work itself out. And that worked.

Quite a few of Richard's mates from St. Edmund's enrolled at TTW, and they learned no longer to rely on the school bell to dictate classes and friendships. They now had to navigate how to be with each other without the supervision and instruction that comes from teachers. They now had Kerry Smyth, Transition to Work coordinator, running the show, and although pint-sized, she was no pushover. Totally invested in getting this program and the kids to maximum potential, she set to work putting in schedules, work placements, and contacts. The focus was on maximizing each student's strengths as well as working to ensure their weaknesses would not restrict their capacity to work. She was totally invested in their futures. As with any new start-up, there were issues, but that was to be expected with something that had grown out of nothing.

Kerry was so passionate about TTW because "TTW allowed young people to be included into mainstream society and to adjust into adult life; and helped parents make that adjustment too."

TTW really focuses on the individual's strengths and weaknesses. It's not a one-shoe-fits-all type of education. It's totally holistic. To help the young people find their vocation, work is done both in group sessions and through individual, one-on-one guidance. Richard much preferred, and learned better through, one-on-one teaching. He could focus more and was distracted less, especially given that his bestie, Michael, was there as well.

The focus was not purely on getting a job. The program also taught basic life skills. The group learned how to prepare meals, how to do their laundry, and how to use money. There was also more adventurous travel training. Part of the push for me with getting a TTW program up and running was to ensure that if Richard wanted someday to have his own place, I wanted him to have the ability to do so. I also wanted him to learn resilience and what to do when mistakes happen. Richard was an "easy option" type of guy. If he could get out of something he would; if he could get someone else to do it, he would; and if someone else wanted to lead, he would follow. Less stress and difficulty that way. But that's not life. I wanted him to understand that and not be afraid of it.

Rich had mastered public transportation in high school, so he was confident about catching trains. He knew how to get around and he was more confident overall, so he would never panic when trains were delayed or canceled. He would calmly find the best solution he could. I loved this, and I celebrated wildly each time he did it. I know that might sound like an overreaction, but having the cognition to navigate what can be, at times, the worst of public transport and not end up in Timbuktu was not only a great relief but something to be really proud of.

~

Over the next two years, several work placements were found by Kerry and her team, which was not always an easy ask. Kerry would often lament about the challenges of convincing companies to take on our young people so that they would have an opportunity to learn on-the-job skills. But she plowed on, and landed Richard and his mates some great positions. It wasn't always a successful fit, but nothing ventured, nothing gained, and when Richard was given the opportunity to do work experience, he totally embraced it. The outcome has been life changing for us all.

What happened over those two years was a blessing and an awakening. Guiltily, enjoying the fact that I didn't have to attend another speech night or swimming carnival, nor do my canteen duties (the school was relieved about that, as I once almost burned down the canteen!), I found having an adult son was becoming an unexpected joy.

Everything that now is was made possible because a group of people decided to simply make it happen. We were all in a good place.

Good fortune hit when a good friend of ours, Andrew Walsh, offered Richard the opportunity of a lifetime. Andrew worked on the Athens Olympic Games, the Rugby World Cup, and the London millennium celebrations, and now he had been asked to direct the opening and closing ceremonies of the 2011 Special Olympics in Athens. Andrew loved and admired people with intellectual disabilities, so this to him was a no-brainer. He asked Richard if he would like to come over and work with him at the Games. Before I knew it, we were planning yet another trip together.

"Where's Athens, Mum?"

"In Greece, which is not far from Malta."

"Greece! Greece! Can we go to see the cast of *Mamma Mia!*, pleeease?"

In 2008 the movie *Mamma Mia!* had been released, and Richard became totally addicted. By the time we were heading to Athens in 2011, he must have seen it a hundred times, and he was madly in love with Amanda Seyfried, the sweet young star of the film. Richard sometimes has a real problem working out fact from fiction; it's a Down syndrome thing. Well, actually I should say it is more about being age appropriate, for although Richard is chronologically an adult, a lot of his abstract thinking is more in keeping with a child's, so he truly believed that the whole cast of *Mamma Mia!* actually lived on the island of Skopelos, where the movie was set.

Given that we were going halfway around the world and I wanted to see more of it, I made a big decision.

"Do you want to go to London, Richard, and maybe add Malta on as well?"

And so we did. The plane trip to London was as excruciating as that first flight to Brisbane all those years ago. Richard on an airplane is relentless. He never stops talking and fidgeting, and the slightest turbulence sets him off. Even so, he loved it, and the cabin crew loved him. I, meanwhile, just wanted it to end.

I had planned excursions to all the *Harry Potter* venues and booked hop-on/hop-off buses. I had told Richard of the riches at the British Museum, the Tower of London, and Buckingham Palace. I'd booked tickets for *Mamma Mia!* the musical. I was pretty sure a week wasn't going to be enough. I gave Richard a copy of the Lonely Planet guide to London on the plane to look at.

"Is there anything you would really like to see?" I asked him.

"Yes, I want to go to that place where they have the heads of all the dead people."

"Umm, not sure I understand what that is, Richard?"

"It's an art gallery, Mum, where they have the pictures of the dead people heads."

"Oh, the National Portrait Gallery."

"Derrr, Mum, yes, that one!"

"What else do you want to see?"

"The Globe Theatre."

What? Where had my son hidden his love of the real arts? Not just crappy movies and pop songs but real theater, real art. I realized then that I had far underestimated Richard. I had pigeonholed him into a simple life with unsophisticated interests. How remiss of me to do that, to just assume there would be no appreciation for aesthetic beauty, for classical music. I needed to change my views, introduce more culture into his life. He clearly appreciated it.

We arrived in London in June. It occurred to me only when we arrived that we would have to battle London peak-hour traffic, so instead of the hassle of the Underground, we made our way to the quieter bus stop. Settled into our hotel rooms, I suggested we have a little nap, wash, and then head out.

After our nap, Richard made an announcement.

"I need to get to Platform 9¾, Mum," he said.

We headed to King's Cross railway station to see where Harry Potter had guided his trolley into the world of Hogwarts, Professor Dumbledore, and He Who Must Not Be Named. I must admit, I was probably just as excited as Richard.

The London Underground is not a place for the fainthearted. How would we manage all those steps, all those people, that mass of intersecting tunnels and escalators as high as a mountain? These were all difficult physical activities that Richard would have to face, and I began to panic. Having lived in London in my younger years, I knew it well, and with the knowledge that it is fast-paced and takes no prisoners, you just have to move. But how would Richard cope? How would all the commuters cope? Well, we coped. Several people stopped and asked if Richard needed help. Men in suits, women in their fashionable heels, skinheads, and Rastas all offered to help if help was needed. Londoners made that trip easy. Richard grew in those few days. He became a little street smart and appreciated that the world is a very big place, with all kinds of people. I saw him blossom with the experience.

Malta was our next stop. Love and family embraced us the whole time we were there. The Maltese are breeders—my grandmother had eighteen children—so there were aunties, cousins, second and third cousins to enjoy; and that was just on my mother's side. Of course, it was never going to be long enough. Our next destination was Athens, where Richard would be working with Andrew. As it turned out, they would also be working amid Greece's mini-revolt against the European Union's austerity measures. I had been worried about London, but this was another step up. Firebombs, police everywhere, civil unrest.

As an organization, the Special Olympics is dynamic. It celebrates the extraordinary achievements of people with disabilities through sport. Eunice Kennedy Shriver started the Special Olympics movement by holding summer day competitions for young people with intellectual disabilities in her backyard in the late 1950s. She saw how unfair it was for these young people not to be included in sporting activities, and rather than focus on what they couldn't do, she focused on what they could. It is said Eunice was inspired by her older sister, Rose Marie, who had an intellectual disability, although the Kennedy family hid it from public view, and the movement is still run by the Kennedy-Shriver family. Special Olympics does what the other Olympic movements do and brings together athletes from around the world to compete in all sorts of sports. Athletes are chosen to represent their countries through merit: you play hard, you get the rewards, just like any other athlete. Often confused with the Paralympic movement, Special Olympics actually holds its games on a different year in a different country. I find this a pity, as I can only see the benefits of holding all three games in the same year and country. The exposure it would give the movements would be amazing, and I have been told conflicting reasons why they are not held jointly. From my understanding, it comes down to politics. It's a shame, as I truly believe that the general public would embrace and celebrate these amazing athletes who not only strive all year round to achieve their personal best but are competitive, break records, and are just as enthusiastic about their chosen sports as any other athletes are.

Richard was not the athletic type; he much preferred the comfort of the lounge and the remote control. However, several of his friends had made it onto the Australian team, which was terrific for our stay in Athens. Harry and Andrew, his friends from St. Edmund's, and his dancing buddy, Mel, were there representing Australia in softball.

Every morning I took Richard to work with Andrew, then we spent the afternoon exploring Athens. We met up with Harry's and Andrew's families in the evening at a Forum square to enjoy amazing food, song, and conversation. We were both wide-eyed. Above all else, what I loved was just enjoying Richard. How he held himself and engaged with people was wonderful to see. People still stared, people still asked questions, but there was a sense that because he was different they were going to make his experience better. When we bought yogurt from the local market, the shop owner gave Richard several to see which he liked the most. He of course chose the creamiest. At our local taverna Richard was always given an extra glass of fresh OJ, and I was given a little extra wine. It wasn't overt, it wasn't discussed, but it was gratefully accepted. It was not about pity; it was about kindness.

Richard loved working with Andrew, although I suspect not a great deal of work was done. His job was in the office, helping with clerical work. I'm sure there was a lot of hanging around, chatting, and looking at the sets. Attending the opening ceremony was a highlight of the trip. VIPs from all over the world came, with countries represented by prime ministers, ambassadors, and politicians. Some countries, small and large, really turned it on, celebrating their teams by showing up and mingling with the athletes. Competition was stiff.

Seeing the Australian team walking in at the opening ceremony threw us all into a frenzy. Richard was so happy to see his friends. We cheered and screamed and carried on like banshees.

With our good friend Alischa, we went on to cruise the Aegean. Sadly, getting to the *Mamma Mia!* island was impossible in the time frame we had. Richard was upset but realistic. Compromise meant that we would do a seven-day cruise. It was my idea of hell, but Richard was determined to cruise, so cruise we did.

"Where to next?" he exclaimed on the plane ride home.

Our trip to the United States in 2013 was fantastic. The plane trip was the usual "Please stop talking: you are driving me crazy." Not offended at all by this, Richard continued to talk, and talk, and talk. He also wanted to watch the same movies as I did, and he again charmed the cabin crew. However, he could now use the toilet without locking himself in. Small mercies. But he also had more plane knowledge than before, having watched the series *Air Disasters*, which led to heightened fear and the awareness that we were essentially falling out of the sky.

During our past travels I had tried to keep the cost to a minimum, but this time I decided we would splurge a little. We would do Los Angeles, Disneyland, and Las Vegas. We would stay in fine hotels. Little did I know, the one I chose in Beverly Hills, the Beverly Hilton, was the place where Whitney Houston had died. But it was a rather splendid hotel and, blessedly, met the very high standards of my young man. Now a seasoned traveler and hospitality industry employee, Richard had started to become a little more critical of certain things: the staff not being as attentive as he would have liked, the burgers not being as good as the ones back home, the taxi driver driving too fast. Unlike my sweet little Richard of yore, this new one was a bit of a complainer. In the two years since our Athens trip, and now age twenty-two, he had changed.

I had noticed it the year before, when we went on a family holiday to Fiji that included my mother, who requires either a Valium or half a bottle of whiskey before she even steps onto a plane. The slightest bit of turbulence set her and Richard off into their respective forms of hysteria. *I* needed a bottle of whiskey by the time we landed four hours later.

"Mum, I don't want to fly back with Grandma anymore; she talks too much and she is scaring me with her screams."

"Benny, I don't want to sit next to Richard anymore; he won't stop talking."

Unbelievable.

In LA, Richard insisted we do the hop-on/hop-off bus. This was his favorite form of travel. "I feel free up here and I can see everything," he would say.

I let him be my guide. Although he was new to his iPad, he really got a grip on what he wanted to do and where he wanted to go. We went from Venice Beach to Rodeo Drive to Universal Studios and so much more. We toured celebrity houses and ate at famous restaurants. Best of all, we went to a Dodgers game. I had booked tickets months ahead of time and worked out that there was a direct bus from our hotel to the "holy land": Dodger Stadium. I have no idea why I like baseball so much. It must have been all those corny movies I watched as a kid and that classic Abbott and Costello routine "Who's on First?" Now, here we were on a bus heading downtown.

Like the London Underground, the bus system in LA is about transporting huge groups of people around the city. I thought this would be a good way for Richard and me to see the real Los Angeles, not just the tourist spots. There are only a few things that make me afraid for Richard's safety. When he was young, I used to tell him that if anyone tried to kidnap him, to just lie down. No one would be able to pick up his deadweight. Other than him being kidnapped, all my other fears were about his health. On our bus trip, we found ourselves sitting opposite a woman who was either mentally unstable or drugged to the eyeballs. I could feel her danger. I put my arm around

Richard, and he, too, inched closer to me. She fixed her stare on Richard and then exclaimed, loudly and aggressively, "What's that sick boy doing on this bus? Get him off. He shouldn't be on my bus."

All eyes were on us. My face was flushing, and Richard started to say something.

"Richard, be calm and don't look at her."

"Mum, she is being rude. What does she mean?"

Feeling confused and belittled in public, he would not let it go.

"She is awful, Mum, and I want to get off the bus."

"He shouldn't be allowed out," the woman continued. "He should be in a home. Ugly little brat."

As she was shouting, she lost her balance, and her groceries fell on the ground. Now she was so angry, she was hissing at us. I made ready to get off the bus. Just as I was about to tell Richard to get ready to move, three or four Latino men and women, all speaking in Spanish, made their way toward us and stood in front of Richard.

"Just don't say anything. She is crazy," said one of the women.

I was getting teary at this point. Richard was pale and nervous. Nothing like this had ever happened to us, not in Australia or London or Fiji or anywhere else. I was more scared than I had ever been. LA is known to be a dangerous place, and I felt its edge that day. All that mattered was protecting my son. These good people had come to the rescue. Someone went up to talk to the driver. He stopped the bus and told the crazy woman to get off, and of course I thanked him.

Richard was clearly upset and kept asking why she had been so mean to him. It's hard sometimes to explain discrimination and cruelty to anyone, let alone to the person who is being discriminated against. It's even harder when it is your own son. Simply telling him the woman was crazy did not wash with him this time.

"Honey, some people have mental health issues," I said, "which means that their brains see things differently than us. She has a lot of issues, she is unhappy, and she probably takes a lot of drugs. You just happened to be the person she was focused on. Now, how about we don't think of that for now and think about the baseball game? Now, that will be fun. Can't wait for that Dodger hot dog!"

But Richard did not bounce back immediately the way he usually did. He was still clearly shaken.

Just before we got to the stadium, he brightened up.

"Guess I will need two Dodger Dogs to get over that woman, Mum."

I breathed a sigh of relief. He was back.

Richard is a big wuss: he hates rides and anything that is remotely dangerous. He's had this fear for many years, even telling me once that he hated me for making him go on a fast waterslide. It was no different when we visited Universal Studios and the Disney California Adventure Park. He almost lost it when Godzilla jumped out at him, and when we sat in at the very popular Bug's Land theater, where the seats actually moved and pinched, he ran screaming out of his chair, hysterical.

"It's not funny, Mum," he said, clearly unimpressed by my laughter.

"Yes it is! You almost wet yourself."

"You're so mean to me."

"Yes, I know!"

Later that day, at Disneyland, I was the one who got the creeps when Richard and I realized that Pluto was following us about. Every turn we made he'd be there, just hanging back a bit. Occasionally he would get quite close and Richard and I would run off. It went from being funny to weird, but we finally lost him. He'd probably found someone else to gawk at. Experiencing something so fabulous with Richard was a real highlight, and I had just as much fun as he did.

Maybe more.

"Mum, you're embarrassing me," commented Rich as I twirled around.

"Why?"

"You keep dancing and singing, and people are staring at you."

"Well, Rich, as your mother it is my job to embarrass you. That's what mothers do."

When I saw Buzz Lightyear, I screamed with excitement. This was the final straw for Richard. He went to sulk on a seat. And that was like a red rag to a bull.

"You know what, mate," I told him, "I have come all this way with you so that you could have a good time, and you're just being a spoiled brat."

"Well, I have asked you not to embarrass me," he retorted.

"Perhaps, Richard, if you just joined in the fun, you wouldn't be embarrassed. Now, either you start smiling or I will leave you here."

As much as I adore Richard, his behavior at times can cause me to ask the question "What have I done?" He knows he can get away with murder, and he does, but rude behavior, no matter his disability, is unacceptable. Balancing his behavioral limitations against what he knows he can get away with had always been a tricky thing. The older he got, the smarter he got at manipulating me. My guilt let him win sometimes, but I wasn't putting up with bad behavior in Disneyland. I started to walk away.

"Okay, Mum, I'm smiling; I'm smiling a lot."

And so, in the end, was I. I got to see Buzz Lightyear, Woody, Slinky, as well as Mickey and Minnie. Woo-hoo! I loved sharing all of that with Rich, and he loved sharing it with me. These wonderful life experiences are a right for everyone, and there should be no limit on what life has to offer, regardless of your intellectual capacity.

Our last stop was Vegas, Sin City, where I had us booked into the Bellagio. I had stayed there once before and just loved it. I knew Rich would too. We were given a fantastic room on the thirty-fifth floor, where the view was spectacular.

Coincidentally, my friend Carolyn and her kids Liz and Jackson were also booked into the Bellagio. Jackson had attended St. Edmund's, and Carolyn and I had been friends ever since Liz had started at Mount Kuring-gai Primary School. We were so excited to be there all together.

Upon arrival, we decided a few drinks by the pool were in order.

I don't think the sight of Richard and Jackson being served cocktails by a rather luscious-looking young woman will ever leave me. Jackson is a handsome six-foot-four-inch guy, and, well, Richard is four-four. They looked a pair. It was priceless: I thought Richard's eyes would pop out of his head. I'm not one to stereotype, but at that moment Richard was like any other man. The waitress was beautiful, and he appreciated that.

We went to shows, we took bad photos, we even played the poker machines, although this caused some issues with the concierge who kept asking me to see Richard's identification.

"You can actually ask him yourself," I said.

The concierge had that "Please rescue me" look that I know so well. "Do you have your ID, young man?" he asked.

Having learned to keep our passports with me, I handed it over.

"Okay, good luck, and have a good time."

"Thanks, we will!" said Richard.

Then we lost our money to the machines. Oh well, next time.

Our daylong tour to the Grand Canyon was breathtaking. The sheer magnitude of the place was overwhelming. I had taken Richard to Uluru many years before, and for once he had stopped talking. He just sat and looked at the rock. He did the same at the Grand Canyon. There is a spirituality in places like that. They deserve a respectful silence, and for whatever reason Richard affords them that quietude. Perhaps my screen-addict son and Mother Nature have made a pact I don't know about. Nevertheless, it leaves me feeling awestruck and truly blessed anytime it happens.

Unfortunately, there is always some loudmouth lurking, ready and waiting to break that meditative bliss. We have all come across them. They know everything, and their experiences are always bigger and better than yours. On our tour was a woman who knew someone who knew someone with Down syndrome, so therefore felt entitled to share her insights, such as "Don't they do well these days?" and "It's so nice to see your son out and about," as if Richard weren't even there.

On the ride back from the canyon I lied and told this woman I had a terrible headache. I had taken two Panadols and needed to close my eyes. She then started talking to Richard. He looked at her and said, "My mum has a headache and she needs quiet, please."

I gave him a wink. He gave me his big smile.

# 9

# Working-Class Man

"We need to make sure that we're all working together
to change mind-sets, to change attitudes, and to fight
against the bad habits that we have as a society."
—JUSTIN TRUDEAU

I didn't want for Rich not to be part of life's big picture. Socrates said, "To be is to do," and Sartre, "To do is to be," and I am not sure which one is right. What I do know is that working is a part of life; it connects you to people and gives you money, and that means independence. For Richard, it was also about being in an environment that would challenge him and open him up to a fuller life and, I hoped, would open him up to so many more opportunities.

After two and a half years in the Transition to Work program, a place was found for Richard to get some further work experience at a hotel pub on Sydney's North Shore. I was so happy Richard got a temporary placement there, as I knew he would enjoy being with people. It was a few train stops away from his father's home, where he was still living. The pub was always busy and had a reputation for a fabulous management and staff. I held my breath, as I was desperate for Richard to get a permanent job out of the experience. Peter, the hotel's manager back then, saw the challenges of work experience:

The step into work experience is challenging—like going on the biggest blind date. You have no idea of the personality or attitude of the candidate, unlike hiring staff when you have a CV or word of mouth from previous employers. When approached about Richie, we were hesitant, as the first time we tried someone in that role, it didn't work out well. So we stepped up to try again and it was the best thing we have done. The transition to permanency was easy and gave us, as well as Richard, a feeling of progress and pride that he had earned the job through hard and dedicated work. So it was like a reward or recognition for both of us.

After several months, Richard was offered a permanent part-time position.

I was so incredibly proud of him: he had achieved this all on his own, and I truly appreciated how hard he had worked to get his job. He was on his feet all day working in the dining area, setting tables and clearing plates and cutlery after people had finished eating; he also worked in the bottle shop breaking up all the cardboard boxes. I find it interesting that when I tell people how Richard got his job all on his own, they say, with every good intention, "Well, he couldn't have done it without you and Graeme," as if we had been standing there helping him at work. I could have thumped the person who said, "Yes, they are lovely, patient people at that pub," as if those without disabilities aren't ever the worst employees. Often, those with disabilities will do everything they possibly can to succeed. They don't take opportunities for granted.

Richard always wanted to work. He saw the benefit of it and just wanted to be like everyone else. He was so proud of getting his uniform and couldn't wait to start, but he was also quite nervous. It took him some time to settle in, and it has not always been smooth sailing. "There have been some tears along on the way, when customers have said things in jest, and [Richard] didn't understand," Peter explains.

"But these incidents were easily resolved. He is so much easier to deal with than other staff, as he genuinely wants to come to work and contribute to the hotel."

Having the backing of a good team helps, from Peter, the hotel owner and Richard's boss, who just adores Richard and has a great relationship with him, to the supportive, caring managers and kitchen and bar staff, who are good colleagues. Rich has made it a rule to get on well with everyone, and his boss has commented that his positive attitude and friendly nature mean customers warm to him immediately.

Although his father and I have always stressed the importance of manners, Richard's success at work was and is not just about manners. It's about an inherent desire to be part of a team and be recognized for who he is and the value of his contribution. I admire him for that, and I like his chutzpah. At times I have worried that he might be excluded.

A few years back, when he was performing in a production with his drama group at the Marian Street Theatre, Richard proudly announced that several of his workmates would be coming to the performance. Marian Street Theatre for Young People runs many programs for abled and disabled performers. Richard loves being with his group and has grown in confidence for being part of this amazing performing troupe.

I was worried that the young people at his work were probably just saying yes to be polite, so I prepared him for the disappointment of the no-shows. On performance day, much to my surprise and joy, ten or so of his mates from work showed up and sat in the front row to support him. I can tell you I shed more than just a few tears at that. Clearly, I underestimated not just the friendships but also the capacity these gorgeous young people had to make a difference, to not be influenced by the discrimination of the past but to truly embrace inclusion.

Since then, Rich has been invited to twenty-first birthday parties, pub crawls, and dinners. At the staff Christmas party, a big event on his social calendar, his popularity is something to behold. A few years back I dropped him off at the North Sydney Oval, where a cricket match had been organized and the guys were in full swing, with many of the girls sitting around in a big circle, chatting away. As soon as they saw Richard approach, several of the girls got up and hugged him and had him sitting and mingling with them in no time at all.

I make a point of not getting out of the car and escorting him anymore when he's with his workmates. I do hang back for a bit and observe—just a little peep to see what the interaction is like. When he was younger, I had heartbreaking moments when I could see he was being excluded. Even now I still feel the urge to rescue him. But I needn't worry any longer. He makes his own friendships and is confident about who he is.

After Richard had been working at the hotel for four years, I got a little worried that he was becoming bored with his job. He talked about leaving and finding something "harder, with more responsibility" and "not so many hours." I love that about him: he has, at times, little in the way of a reality check. Or maybe he does. I guess I would like those things from a job too. Luckily, the hotel management also sensed that he was getting bored and started making some changes to his daily routine. It paid off in spades.

One of the jobs he was given was answering the phone. *Really? My boy with Down syndrome was asked to answer the phone?* Of course, I cried. Managers Matt and Jono just treat him like everyone else. One time Peter had to step away for ten minutes. Richard offered to fill in for him and said, "I will sit down at your desk and do your job, Pete." Rich is now the longest-serving employee at the pub—some achievement.

Then there are the pub regulars. They tease him, encourage him, and treat him like a mate. He is part of their world. There have been times when we have been out shopping or in a café and I'll see a person smiling and walking toward us. I'll think, *Gee, I don't know this person,* and then a hand will shoot out.

"G'day, mate, nice to see you."

"Hi, Greg, I'm out shopping. This is my mum."

"Ya got a good kid there, Mum. See ya at the pub tomorrow, Rich."

"Yep, see you then."

"Who was he?" I'll ask curiously.

"Just a mate from the pub."

So he now has people in his life whom I don't know. Part of me likes this, and at other times it scares me. Is it all right for him to have friends who are adults who are not part of my circle, or his father's circle, and have therefore not been vetted by either of us? I guess it has to be that way. While I worry over Richard's vulnerability, he is not naïve.

Well, sometimes he is.

"Mum, guess what?"

"What?"

"I won fifteen dollars."

"How did you win fifteen dollars?"

"I backed a horse."

"You what?"

"I got a hot tip from one of the blokes in the pub, and I backed a horse."

"How much did you put on it?"

"Fifteen."

"Well, then you didn't win anything. And how many times have I told you gambling is bad?"

"Well, you back horses in the Melbourne Cup."

"Well, yes, but that is only once a year."

"But you lose every year."

Now the logic is back and working against me.

"Don't change the subject. You put down fifteen and you got back fifteen, so you won nothing. You just got your money back."

"But I actually won fifteen."

"Well, yes, you won it, but you also lost it."

And on it goes. We did the whole thing of taking fifteen dollars out of the wallet and putting it in one hand and then swapping it to the other. It made no difference. He was just pumped up he'd won fifteen dollars. The pub has poker machines—pokies—and a TAB (an off-track betting agency) and people go to the pub to place a bet or pop a few dollars in the poker machines, so I thought he might be used to the logistics of winning and losing.

It was different when a bet was lost over football and his favorite team.

"Hi, Mum. Please don't get angry with me, but I gambled again."

"What? I have told you, Richard, you will lose money."

"Ah, but I didn't lose money."

"What do you mean you didn't lose money?"

"I had a bet about the football and bet one of the blokes at work that the Bunnies would beat the Bulldogs and I lost, so I have to wear the Bulldogs T-shirt."

As cranky as I was with him, it did make me laugh. What it said was that this kid just wants to be out there; he just wants to be treated like everyone else, with all the risks and consequences that life brings. Who was I to put a stop to it? It's a joy that people don't feel sorry for him, pity him, or treat him differently. I am glad that the guy in the pub made him stick to the bet. I'm glad that he learns lessons and makes his own choices. I'm glad that he is a young man with purpose and strength of character who can hold his own in any company. He has done that.

Employment opportunities for people with intellectual disabilities are limited, and it is an ongoing source of frustration for many parents that their kids can't get rich and rewarding work. For someone with an intellectual disability, finding meaningful work—or any sort of work, for that matter—has traditionally been fraught. Just as the idea that people with Down syndrome could and should have access to education didn't come to fruition until the last part of the twentieth century, so the idea that they can and should be able to work in open employment is a battle still being fought.

Here's the thing: it's like anyone else in the workplace. You have great employees, average employees, and some dreadful ones. I can't say for certain that a person with an intellectual disability will make a great employee. Some just don't. But after seeing how well Richard was doing, I believe people with intellectual disability can work hard, be the most punctual employees, and totally commit to their employer.

The system fails because the right jobs are not matched to the right people. Once Richard was given work experience in a video rental shop. His hours were from 10:00 a.m. till 12:00 p.m.—the quietest time of the day. The manager working there was a goth who looked like he would murder anyone who walked into the store. Richard was bored, as he had no one to interact with and was scared shitless of the possible serial murderer he was working with. So, *surprisingly*, the job didn't work out!

Conversations vary among my friends who have kids with intellectual disabilities. Some are more than happy for their kids to work in "assisted employment," the new term for sheltered workshop, and some really want their kids to be in open employment. Again, for me it is about the choice—not the choice of the parent but the choice of the person with an intellectual disability. Assisted employment is fine; it's great to have any job, if that's what you want. It offers a social environment that suits some people with intellectual disabilities. For others, it's not right.

But the question for me is "Why aren't there more opportunities in open employment?" It's not hard. Yes, it takes some work, and, yes, it does take some adjusting; but if an employer really put their mind to it, a job can be created or modified to suit that person's needs. I know of a place, a factory, that makes very small things to fit into computers. It's fiddly work that requires concentration and total focus. The management worked out that the people best suited for this job would be people who are autistic. *Bingo*: win-win! That's smart thinking.

The team at Richard's pub understand that there are some things

Richard can't do, but they make sure to give him tasks that satisfy him and make him feel good about himself.

One of the regulars decided after seeing Richard at work that he would hire a person with an intellectual disability at his business. He was always worried about taking on a person with an intellectual disability—chalk it up to his fear of the unknown—but after watching Richard and seeing how much joy he brings to the place, he was no longer worried. I wish more people had his attitude.

# 10

# Love and Ashley

"There is only one happiness in this life, to love and be loved."
—GEORGE SAND

"Love recognizes no barriers. It jumps hurdles, leaps fences, penetrates walls to arrive at its destination full of hope."
—MAYA ANGELOU

"Hi, Mum."

"Hi, honey, what are you up to?"

"I'm talking to you!"

For years he had said this, and for years I had explained with some exasperation that that was not what I meant.

"Okay, other than talking to me, what else is happening to you?"

"I have something really exciting to tell you. I asked Ashley to be my girlfriend, and she said yes. I'm so happy."

I wondered about this. Had she not just broken up with her old boyfriend?

"Well, that's lovely, and I hope you two will be happy."

"Oh, we will be!" he assured me.

After successfully completing some wonderful steps toward living a full life of joy and independence—learning to get from place to place on his own, getting a high school diploma, securing and maintaining a job, cultivating his own friendships—Richard was now heading into the next phase of his adult life, and it was one I was not quite ready for.

He'd had a girlfriend when he was in high school, and she was sweet, but it was not a relationship he was entirely happy with. It had caused him some pain, as she was quite bossy. (The irony, of course, is that his mother is bossy.) Bossiness brings on stress for Richard. There were times when he would be in tears because he was unsure about how to end the relationship. He eventually did, and he learned a lot from it. He learned that he does not have to do something he doesn't want to do to make someone else happy. He learned that he had a voice and it was okay to have his own views. He learned that it was okay to let someone go as long as you were kind and caring in doing so. But he was still emotionally young.

Here's the thing: although Rich wanted to have a girlfriend and a relationship that was meaningful and rewarding, I didn't feel he was quite capable of that—at least, not a relationship he could develop in the way most of us without a disability do (although I am mindful of my own relationship failure rate even as I write this, and perhaps it is why a solid relationship has been so important to Richard).

Did he have the capacity to take on a relationship with all that comes with it: the drama, the stress, the disappointments? On reflection, I should have respected his desires and needs more than I did. He is, after all, a man, regardless of his disability, which did not curb his need for love and affection, or his desire for intimacy. As with most of us, love is important, and I believe it is also necessary.

I was out of my comfort zone with Richard's new phase.

As soon as Richard started high school, Ashley had befriended him with the intention of being friends. They liked each other; it was a friendship based on being happy in each other's company. Ashley does not have Down syndrome. She has a different type of intellectual disability, a developmental delay of unknown cause. She is a whiz on the computer and has a relentlessness about her that, on a good day, you are so grateful for and applaud, but on a bad day you could lovingly throttle her for. She wants to include people in her life and at times can be overwhelmingly insightful and truthful. She is honest and kind and, above all, she really loves my son. So when Richard popped the "Will you be my girlfriend?" question, she was dizzy with excitement. I was genuinely happy for them both.

I had known Ashley's parents, Lorraine (not to be confused with Richard's stepmother) and John, for some time, so getting to know the family wasn't difficult. Parents who have kids with an intellectual disability have many challenges, not the least of which is the matter of "Are we all on the same page?" if and when their children want to enter into a romantic relationship. Sometimes it works brilliantly, while at other times there's a profound objection by one or both parties. A big "No, it's not going to happen" is, I believe, a pity. Lucky for us, we all agreed we wanted our kids to have a relationship that was supported not just by both sets of parents but also their extended families.

Being intellectually disabled, Richard and Ashley needed a lot of guidance through their romance, and not just through the complicated emotional obstacles that can come up between all couples. They needed help with the basic logistics: deciding on when and where to meet for dates and how they were going to get there. If they went to the movies, they could usually manage by themselves during the day; but if they wanted to go out for dinner, it generally meant a parent would need to step in.

Since both Ashley and Richard came from large families, a lot of the dates involved many family members. It was a bit like the courtship of Toula and Ian in My Big Fat Greek Wedding: where they went, we went. I worried that staff at restaurants or movie theaters would not quite get them, but generally people were really encouraging and helpful. Sometimes a phone call would be made just to ensure that the staff knew they might need a little help.

Managing schedules, including their individual work and social commitments, was a challenge, as was the fact that Ashley was on a bus route and Rich caught trains, and they lived forty minutes away from each other.

The good thing was that there was no young adult awkwardness, no jealousy or hidden agendas when they were together. From the beginning, they had a mutual understanding of what a relationship should be like, and it was almost old-fashioned. They would have their dates, and if they did have a sleepover, they would sleep in separate rooms. They would have sweet little calls and buy each other loving gifts.

As a publisher I published many self-help books and eventually studied to be a counselor. I counsel a lot of couples and as I say to them, "You need to have each other's back, celebrate each other's strengths, and talk about your weaknesses." Rich and Ashley certainly had each other's back, sometimes to an annoying degree, especially when Ashley would defend Rich after I'd admonished him for making a bad decision. Soon after becoming his girlfriend, she started to take ownership of my son, and I didn't like it one bit. It was certainly not what I had expected, because I did not think she would have the capacity to have those feelings of dedication and loyalty, or even the courage to tick me off. But she did. As a result, I was forced to acknowledge that these two young people were forging a separate connection all their own.

Some issues seemed insurmountable at the time. There were difficulties with communication when neither could truly articulate what they wanted, or needed, from the other. There were assumptions on what a boyfriend or girlfriend should do. Richard, being an only child, was used to getting his own way. Ashley wanted her mother involved in every decision that was made. Others were small things, insignificant to us but hugely significant to Rich and Ashley. The one thing that really made me laugh was sharing food. Richard is not a good sharer at the best of times, and Ash was happy to have a taste of his meal. He would begrudgingly let her try the very smallest, and I mean very smallest, morsel.

I know all of Richard's behavior signals, good and bad. He is my son; I know his quirks, his language, his soul, and his spirit. I had to learn Ashley's little ways. Rightly enough, she has her own set of quirks, her own language, soul, and spirit. As Richard and Ashley grew and their relationship changed, so, too, have their families needed to adapt along with them. It can be hilarious, at other times exhausting, but it is never dull.

>

After four years of courtship, Rich and Ashley decided they wanted to move into an apartment together on their own. They had often slept at each other's homes, where they eventually did share their beds, and they spent many weekends and holidays together as well, so they were used to each other's idiosyncrasies. Both Ashley's parents and Graeme and I had various views on subject. My main concern was whether I had done enough to prepare our son for this next step. As the mother of an only child, and an only boy child at that, I had been—let's face it, still am—a total pushover when it comes to doing things for Richard. Just in case I wasn't aware of this, he would often say to me, "Mum, I don't know why you pretend to say no: you always give in." Even his mate Michael will say, "Benny, I don't know why you ask us to do stuff, as we know you will do it anyway." After which they both fall about laughing.

As much as I tried to teach Rich self-reliance and independence, I know I wasn't as disciplined as I should have been. His stepmother, Lorraine, was much better at getting him to do domestic duties and preparing him for life outside the family home. She guided him to help around the house and do his fair share. Since I only had Richard on the weekends and holidays, I would often let things slide as long as he at least brushed his teeth and had the occasional wash. As he got older, I began to enforce more responsibility. However, as hard as I tried, he knew how to win me over with "Oh, Mum, while you're going upstairs, can you take this up for me?" or "I really promise to do it tomorrow." Of course, tomorrow would never come.

When it was clear my second marriage was failing, I'd moved to Sydney and taken out a one-year lease on an apartment just next door to my sister Lu, which was a gift in more ways than one. If I was ever out of the house, Rich could be in the apartment on his own with the security of having his adoring auntie next door. He flourished as a result of having time in the apartment on his own, and for the first time I'd begun to imagine him living independently someday. I started putting some "domestic" plans into shape. I knew I was a pushover so I rallied a few people to help Richard get ready for the transition into independence. Lucy and Nick both came over at various times in the week to take Richard shopping or get him to do his laundry. He reluctantly worked on his skills, the payoff being that he would gain necessary abilities for when he had his own place. Little did I think that his first move would be with a girl!

Finding an apartment for them that ticked all the boxes was necessary for success. If we did not put all the right ingredients into this big new pot, we would surely get burned. It had to work not only for Rich and Ashley but also for the three families involved. I believed that one of the key ingredients for this move to be a success was to live in a place that was close to things young people like to do. It had to be easy for them to go shopping, to go to the movies, to get to work easily, to catch trains that would take them places, and also be a place where they could meet friends and just hang out. We found the right apartment, in the right suburb, with all the right requirements. Woo-hooo!

We were all so excited when the big day came. It was a little chaotic, as it was just before Christmas, it was hot (we are upside down in this part of the world), and, sadly, Richard's much beloved grandma was sick in the hospital. But just watching the way Richard walked toward his apartment made me feel so sure that this was right for him. He was taking ownership of his life. I was watching him closely that day; watching for that look of uncertainty or discomfort that sometimes appears. I saw nothing. When Richard is confident about a decision he has made, he never wavers from putting his energy into making it a success. I felt so incredibly proud of him. It was a day of celebration.

His auntie Sue noticed the change as well:

> As Richard has matured I have seen his confidence grow. I was very apprehensive when Richard and Ashley moved into their own home, but I was surprised to see how well Richard coped and how competent he has been. He had no misgivings, as he expected that everything would fall into place and is quietly confident and in many ways very brave. He has a very positive attitude and he doesn't think he can't do things (unless of course he doesn't want to—like exercise!)

The biggest issue for them was the same issue that faces most young couples, and that is coming to terms with the fact that what worked in your family of origin might not be the same as that of your partner's. How we clean a domestic space or make the bed, what we eat, what we watch—all that can be very different. What I didn't want was for Richard to assume the traditional male role and expect that Ashley would be the domestic goddess. I had let him get away with so much that I was worried he would assume Ashley would look after him.

I was relieved and fortunate that Ashley's mum put routines in place and worked with Richard and Ashley to maintain a roster of duties. She created opportunities for them to have their own personal needs met and to ensure that they lived in a safe environment. This part of their lives is ongoing. They need assistance with daily living, but as they grow as a couple, so does their capacity for gaining independence.

Since Australia introduced the National Disability Insurance Scheme (NDIS) in July 2013, the lives of people with intellectual disabilities have been significantly improved. Well, at least, I think so. With the funds available through this program, I can now employ people to help Richard surpass some of the milestones he's been yearning for but that require a huge commitment from someone willing and able. He would kill to learn how to cook (which I have no patience for), go nightclubbing (which I'm too old for), and travel longer distances on his own (I would love him to get to his auntie's place without me).

Very shortly we will be coming up to three years of living together. I say "we," as I feel we have all been living through this together. Communication is key, and we have had some sticky moments; although our children have become good communicators, they occasionally get a bit muddled with plans and decisions. They also get stuck in their ways and don't like to be told what to do. "We are adults, Mum," I might be told: *Back off.* For so many years I have thought that I knew what was best for Rich—that I had his best interests at heart—but now I am realizing that I need to let him make mistakes. I need to let him be disappointed like the rest of us and not get what he wants all the time. But that's easier to write about than to put into practice.

There is also the issue of three women running a household. This is where I sometimes slip up and let my stubbornness take over. Often I will do something one way, but Ashley knows her mother likes it done another way, and so we argue. I get obstinate. She gets upset. We usually compromise, but I am also aware that Ashley has an intellectual disability and at times I just need to let her have her own way. If I stepped back from these scenarios and asked myself why I behave like this, it is because I want my son's ironing to be done the way I like it; I want his towels to be folded the same way as mine, with the tea towels in the third drawer. Everyone in my family stores their tea towels in their third drawer. It's as stupid as it sounds: territorial markings and the stuff of all the mother-in-law jokes created the world over since the dawn of time. The real issue is, of course, that I am not respecting the fact that this is not my home; it is theirs. And if Richard doesn't give a toss about how things are done—and I am sure Ashley's mother, Lorraine, has no issues, either—then neither should I. I never said I was perfect. Far from it. At this point I am still a work in progress in letting things slide.

Importantly, though, they do actually keep their apartment tidy and clean. They are proud of that, and the older they get, the more aware they become of what needs to be done to maintain their home. We are now all in a pretty good routine, with all parents contributing to the smooth running of the household. We try to keep a schedule, and sometimes it works and other times we are all flexible to ensure that the couple are succeeding. The NDIS has certainly helped. We have people who come in to assist with running the apartment and help with cooking skills, cleaning, outings, and exercise regimes. In fact, it has been a blessing, as that regular input from others outside the family seems to encourage the kids to up their game even more. As they have become more comfortable in their home, they've had friends come over for dinner, and Richard has had Michael and their other friend Alex stay over. Like any young couple, they have time apart. Ashley will go off and do her thing and stay over at her mum's, and Richard will take that opportunity to have a boy's night, watching far too much sport, talking about bloke stuff, and having a fabulous time.

Over the last three years, there have not been too many times where I have thought this wasn't going to work—although there have been plenty of tears, mine included. The difficulties usually arise from issues with communication, which, as I said, is the key to success. Both Richard and Ashley needed to adjust to sharing their space, thinking forward, and also (the hardest of all) separation from their families of origin. I could tell when things were not right with Richard, but it would take some probing to find out what exactly was happening. He felt deeply when Ashley was upset or if anyone was being disrespectful to them both. He was determined to be treated as an adult, not to have decisions taken away from him or not to be consulted. For both of them this was probably the most challenging adjustment to make: they wanted to own their own destiny. I know at times that I certainly overstepped the decision-making for them, feeling I knew best. And sometimes I did. But I learned pretty quickly that they both wanted to have a say in their lives. As the weeks and months went by, those challenges became fewer and fewer, the tears dwindled, and there has been much laughter, joy, and happiness as well.

Recently I needed to stay with them at their apartment and didn't arrive until relatively late. I walked into a very clean apartment and dinner was waiting for me, along with a very welcome glass of red wine. I was so impressed. How thoughtful and considerate of them both! After dinner and a bit of chitchat I was looking to make up my bed, when I saw in my little room that the linens had already been turned down and a glass of water placed on the bedside table. Even the lamp had been turned on. At that moment my heart was so full. Through lots of work, determination, and adaptability, Richard and Ashley had made a home for each other. They had made a home for me as well.

Ashley's parents, Lorraine and John, acknowledge that things haven't always been easy. "Yes, they will need assistance in some areas for the rest of their lives. Yes, all the hard work is worth it. The alternative of having no one to love is much more profound. Richard and Ashley have always enjoyed each other's company and show a deep affection for each other. If everyone could be as happy as Richard and Ashley are together, life would be grand."

❧

"Do they have sex?"

Now, there's an inappropriate question. Yet people ask it. I wonder if they would like to know if *I* have sex? Do they ask the parents of other young couples who live together if they have sex? Because these young adults have intellectual disabilities, it seems that people think it is okay to ask this question. I can only respond to this sort of inquiry out of respect for Rich and Ashley, who are both relatively high-functioning adults with intellectual disabilities. So my answer is that they are entitled to the life they want and to conduct it how they want within the bounds of safety and respect for each other. What I have tried to teach Richard is that he needs to respect his partner's wishes and that she needs to respect his.

As for their future, they want to get married; they want to have a life together. Richard wants to have children. Ashley doesn't. What do I think? I wish they could have a family, but they cannot, as they don't have the capacity to look after children on a daily basis. Ashley knows this. Richard is getting there. Were it to happen, Graeme, Lorraine, John, and I would become parents, not grandparents, and we are all too old for that.

I am sad for Rich that one of his life's ambitions will not happen. We talk about it very openly, with me pragmatically explaining the amount of work it takes and the financial and social burdens of being a parent. All of which he gets, but it is still a longing. He places a lot of love on his godson, Charlie, whom he says will be the son he can't have.

I sometimes jokingly say that, together, Rich and Ashley make the perfect person. One's strengths and weaknesses are the other's weaknesses and strengths. They help each other. When others struggle to understand Rich, Ashley translates. She helps him with his buttons and his shaving, and reminds him he has his shirt on backward. She is his other eye. He, in turn, gives her a quiet stability when she is upset and encourages her to step outside her comfort zone. Sometimes they are disrespectful to each other and can be rude and uncaring. Then they hold hands, kiss, and hug. They talk about their lives, make plans to travel, and look forward to attending social events together.

Richard loves and adores Ashley. Ashley loves and adores Richard. He calls her "babe"; she calls him "bub." They giggle, laugh, talk, fight, negotiate, compromise, respect, encourage, and temper one another, and they have each other's backs. They champion their relationship and their love. How lucky are they to have that?

"What do you love about Ashley?" I asked Richard one day.

"She makes me very happy; she loves me a lot; she makes me laugh a lot; she makes me stuff; she comes with me to family stuff."

"And what do you love about Richard, Ashley?"

"He makes me feel very happy and very special; he's nice and cuddly; he's a nice boyfriend; he looks after me and I look after him; he takes me out for dinner."

# 11

# Bright Blue Skies

"I never said I wanted a 'happy' life but an interesting one. From separation and loss, I have learned a lot. I have become strong and resilient . . . We don't even know how strong we are until we are forced to bring that hidden strength forward."

—ISABEL ALLENDE

Richard is now twenty-eight years old. He has a great job, a nice apartment, a woman who loves him, and family and friends who adore him. He is inherently a beautiful soul. He is kind beyond belief and is often the first person to laugh. He can also be a cranky-pants, selfish, and inconsiderate. He is just like the rest of us. However, as he grows and gains confidence in his place in the world, he seems to find life easier. I have learned to find it easier too. I still worry for his safety and his health. I still fixate on worst-case scenarios, which at times makes me feel sick to my stomach, causes me to wake in the middle of the night, and brings tears to my eyes.

Twenty-eight years ago, I made a pact with God. Today, Richard can talk an ear off, he can read, and thank goodness all his bodily self-care is well looked after. But the larger question I've always had—and the one that plagued me for so many years—was whether he would have a "normal" life. What I've discovered is that everyone has a different measure of "normal." It depends on individual life experience.

What I consider normal is probably not the same for a rock star, an international money baron, or an electrical engineer. I might have different standards from someone living in Iowa, Italy, or Indonesia. Everyone has their normal. Their family normal, their work normal, their private normal.

My life with Richard is our normal. We are happy in that normal, as that's the only normal we have. I am aware that in the past I failed to recognize that what other people think of Richard shouldn't matter. If they want to judge, criticize, or assume, they can do that, but as his parent I should not have given it a thought. I should have only considered what was best for Richard. I didn't always do that and made some pretty bad decisions as a result. But as my sister Martha says, "We do what we do at the time," and I did what I did at the time thinking it was the best. Leaving Richard and moving overseas was probably not the smartest thing I have ever done, and I can put in a lot of buts, but I don't want to. It is what it is.

I have asked Richard several times how my living overseas impacted him and what his feelings were about it. It was probably a really hard question to answer, but he has an ability to put things simply, and he is very forgiving.

"I know you always loved me, Mum."

And that's enough. I have apologized for the hurt I caused him, but he didn't seem to think there *was* any hurt. Fortunately, those days are behind us and we have developed a rich, rewarding relationship that grows in strength and stature as each day goes by.

I enjoy not being an outsider anymore. Being on the outside looking in only affords you time, and safety, but it disconnects you. My life was never fully connected with others, nor did I find it had true meaning. It's like you can't be truly present. I chose to be an outsider in both Normal World and Disability World. It was easier not to fully engage in either, as it kept me safe; and although I would occasionally have my outbursts and terribly black days, I didn't want anyone to see what I was feeling in the privacy of my own fear—and I certainly never wanted Richard to feel it, either. Sometimes I would let down my guard and engage. I thought I had transcended the expectation of hurt only to be plunged into that sickening space of defending my child and our existence. It was easier to not venture too deep into conversations about expectations and disability. For someone who is supposedly an "extrovert," I kept a lot of stuff about myself pretty close. I guess by writing this book I am not keeping anything close at all anymore. But as the village grew, so did my confidence and resolve to just enjoy Richard for who he is and not what I had wanted him to be.

Would I change any of Richard? No: he would not be Richard if I did. Down syndrome does not define who he is; instead, it's the values he lives by and the love and kindness he shows to others in his life. Of course, saying Down syndrome doesn't matter would not be truthful, but does it affect his soul? I don't think so. I am so grateful he is here.

When Richard was born, his life expectancy was not good. The medical world told me he wouldn't live past thirty. I lived with that horror for many years. But all these years later I now know that Richard will live a long life. Perhaps not as long as most of us, but as modern medicine improves and Richard's health issues are addressed when they arise, he could live into his sixties, and more than one in ten adults with Down syndrome will live to be seventy. I know Richard will be one of those people. Yay. Most adults with Down syndrome will live longer than we ever thought possible. Families are much better at having our voices heard than ever before.

❧

Recently, I watched the YouTube coverage of Frank Stephens, a long-time Down syndrome advocate who happens to have also been born with the genetic disorder, speaking to a congressional committee in Washington, DC, about genetic testing and the quality and funding for Down syndrome research in the United States. Addressing those who believed fetuses diagnosed with Down syndrome should be aborted, he said, "I am a man with Down syndrome and my life is worth living. I completely understand that people pushing this particular 'final solution' are saying that people like me shouldn't exist . . . Is there really no place for us in this world?"

He said that if there had been genetic testing when he was born, he wouldn't be here today, doing what he's doing. He is a high achiever, a successful actor, and an activist for social justice. He just happens to have a disability. It's something I'd like everyone to watch. Google him. He's inspiring.

Anyone who is fan of *American Horror Story* will be familiar with actress Jamie Brewer, who, in season three, plays the teenage character Nan. Jamie is amazingly talented and also has Down syndrome. In one episode, four teenage girls hang over a balcony in the house they have just moved into and spy on a handsome young man working in his garden next door. The next day the young man turns up at the girls' house, delivering a cake. The slim blonde with attitude immediately assumes the cake is for her and holds out her hands to receive it. But the young man offers the cake to Nan. He doesn't do it out of pity, either. He likes her personality. There's a hint of romance there as well. It's quite refreshing. Google that one too.

I have observed over the years the discussion on the issue of prenatal testing and termination of fetuses with Down syndrome. I have asked myself many times what I would have done had I known early on in my pregnancy. I have no answer. I do, however, find the hypocrisy of the medical community astonishing at times. Many doctors provide so much bad information regarding the "doom and gloom" of having a child with Down syndrome but say nothing of the challenges that some premature babies will have to face in life after doing everything in their power to keep them alive.

We have so many options today, from supermarket shelves to holiday resorts. Choice is everywhere. Except when you're pregnant. The pressure to undergo prenatal testing is enormous, whether you want it or not, and the decision about whether you will have a child with a disability is greatly influenced by the obstetrician. Back in 1991, I was not pressured into prenatal testing. However, I have often considered whether my obstetrician willingly kept quiet regarding his concerns about my pregnancy because he was a religious man. I will never know. What I do know is that I would never have terminated an eighteen-week-old baby.

Yes, it is a struggle having a child who is different; yes, it can cause family hardship; and, yes, it can make you cry and despair beyond belief. But I am a firm believer, now more than ever, that each life is to be valued and celebrated.

My life with Richard has been both beautiful and difficult. The difficulties stem from the choices *I* made, not the ones *he* made. Nor the ones others have made. In all of this life, Richard has been nothing but his true, authentic self. The beautiful words that people have said about him are to his credit, not mine.

People have said to me, "Oh, you and Graeme have done such a good job of raising Richard. He is lucky to have you." *No,* I think. I *am the lucky one to have* him. I know Graeme feels the same. I also know it was not just Graeme and me who helped Richard achieve his amazing success but the communities of loving souls around us who have embraced, nurtured, and respected Richard throughout the years. In return, Richard has given back tenfold. Each of our lives has been enriched by this young man. Through him, we have all learned the true meaning of acceptance. We have all discovered that there is a fine line between ability and disability. Whatever we lack, the loving people around us will cover.

I pray that I have been, and still am, the mother Richard deserves. Richard rarely refers to any disability in his life. He is rich with love and happiness, and he is bursting with optimism. To meet this young man, is to meet someone who is funny, kind, loving, wise, generous, stubborn, and so much more. If you had a collective of Richards, I think it would be called "a smile of Richards."

So when you meet someone who has just had a baby with Down

syndrome, don't say "Sorry." This is the last thing a new parent wants to hear. Reserve "Sorry" for those occasions where it is appropriate. Congratulate the new parents on the birth. I'm not sorry I have a loving, caring, funny, beautiful son.

Last year I was at a Down Syndrome New South Wales board meeting, which was held in Parramatta, in Western Sydney, a few hours' drive away from my place. I had been a board member for only a few months, and the meeting went on forever (as they do), and it was getting quite late. One of the young dads, also a board member, asked me if I was driving back home.

"Oh, no," I said. "I'm staying at Richard's."

He looked at me, incredulous, and it suddenly struck me.

"You know, I never thought I would ever say those words."

Years ago, I might have accepted that Richard would be staying with me. Forever. Now he has everything set up for his independence, including the ability to have his mother stay with him.

Two years ago we went to an ABBA festival in the middle of nowhere. Trundle is remote—think backwater Arkansas—with a population of about three hundred. On the first weekend in May the town explodes with glitter, sequins, wigs, and a big dose of fun. The place is literally invaded by grown men and women dressed as the Swedish foursome. Even the Swedish consulate attended. Rich decided that he would enter the singing competition with his karaoke version of "Dancing Queen." Now, Richard can't sing for toffee, but up he got onstage and belted out an unforgettable performance. He won the hearts of many and also won a prize for best new talent. He became a minor celebrity that night. People chatted with him and encouraged him to come back next year for a repeat performance. Watching that young man engage with people on his own, with nothing to do with me, brought me smiles, laughter, and pure joy. It was infectious. People around him were embracing the happiness that was Richard. Letting him stand alone, not interfering in exchanges between him and strangers, as I have said, is not easy; but the older Richard gets, and the more his own personality shines, the more at ease I am with what is, and should be, a fundamental acceptance of all differences. There's something about seeing a "normal" fifty-year-old guy in a green Lycra jumpsuit, complete with blond wig, full beard, and a beer gut, referring to himself as Anni-Frid while talking to a little guy with a terrible voice, who also happens to have Down syndrome, under a full moon in the middle of nowhere.

The world is a strange, diverse, accepting, and beautiful place, indeed.

# Acknowledgments

Whenever I buy a book, the first thing that I do is look at the acknowledgments. For me, I get a real sense of who is involved in the author's life—who was in, who was left out—and I like to get a feel for the person writing the book. I know: it's weird. Acknowledgments can be a bit like the equivalent of the Academy Award–winning speech. Some are boringly long, and others so short you feel a bit cheated. And as with any speech, you can never really say in full how thankful you really are to those who help and love you.

From little things, big things grow, and what was an innocent conversation with my good friend Judith Curr about this book became a reality. Judith, then publisher at Atria, suggested I write about Richard and me because stories like this should be told. Thank you, Judith, for making this book happen. I was put in the fabulous editorial hands of Daniella Wexler. Thank you, Daniella, Loan Le, Haley Weaver, and the rest of the team for backing this book, making me feel that what I was saying was worth saying. Thank you, Lourdes Lopez, for being so patient with all my crazy questions and for getting me sorted.

Frankly, I am not a great writer: I write like I speak. So, to get this book to a place that made sense, I have four amazing women to thank. These women are all incredibly talented and passionate about words and books, and each one gave me courage to make this book the best it could be, wisdom to make me reflect, and brilliance to make my words shine. But on top of all of that fabulousness, these women, with their beautiful souls and insights, really got what I wanted to say about intellectual disability and, more importantly, about Richard. Thank you all so very much. Firstly, Joanne Tuscano: you saved my sanity by stepping in when I was drowning. You turned this book around. Thank you. Sarah Branham: I love that you got what I wanted to say, brought out the best in my writing, asked some tough questions and made me be better. KC Gibbs: what a pleasure it has been working with you. Thank you for making me trust in what I was saying, for making this book something special, for keeping me from doubting myself and my words, and for making me laugh out loud. And lastly, the fountain of all knowledge Tracylee Arestides: thank you so very much for your counsel, your understanding of all the ins and outs of Down syndrome, and just for being a totally beautiful and inspiring woman.

I asked a lot of people to write testimonials about how they saw Richard. I wanted to see how others viewed him, as everyone has a relationship with him that is unique to them. I also wanted to see what others remembered, since at times my memory was not so sharp. As the book took shape I could not use all those testimonials, so I just want to say a big thank-you to all who wrote one. I am sorry I couldn't use your words, but thank you. In no particular order: Anthea and Michael Karseboom, Carolyn Abrahams, Helena Elms, Louise Long-hurst, the Van den Bergs, Sean and Karyne Gough, Carla Unicomb, Peter Bromley, Cathy Laing, Cathy Burke, Lucy Desoto, Deborah Tobias, Sally Gulson, Karen McEwen, Kerry Smyth, Juliet Rogers, Nettie Locke, Judy Welsh, Karen Carragher, Helen Thornton, Robin Treloar, Sue Cairns, and Anna Hutchinson. And from Richard's pub: James, Treden, Brian, and Peter. To the owners and management of the pub, Peter, Matt, Jono: thank you. You guys have such beautiful hearts.

I am very grateful to Richard's dad, Graeme, and his wife, Lorraine. Thank you for your help, your support, and your words. It means a great deal. Big thanks to Gaye, Bruce, Brigette, and Zoe for reminding me of some very funny moments. And even though you are no longer with us, Nan, thank you for being the most amazing nan ever!

Richard does love Ashley, and so do I. Thanks, Ash, for being a wonderful partner for Richard. Thank you, Lorraine and John, for all you do.

"Mum, family first"—that's Richards motto. This means that if I umm and ahh about attending a family function, I have no choice but to go. Family is very important to both of us. Families are made of many layers, and ours is made of layers of love and joy and support and goodness and kindness. I feel so truly blessed to have you all in my life. So thank you to you all: Martha and Graham, Mari-Luise and Krisztina, Sue and David, Carly and Matt, Melanie and Chris, Faith and Agistino, Chloe and Ben, Tom and Courtney, and those amazing little people that bring so much joy to our lives—Ruby, Finnegan, Charlie, Isla, Molly, and Archer. And, Dad and Mum, I know you are not here in person, but I know you are with me all the time.

I spent many days and nights alone in Wollombi, but I was never really alone, as I always had my two faithful, loyal, and loving dogs, Winston and Nero, with me. You protected and looked after me. You sat by my feet as I wrote and helped me through some pretty dark days. I miss you both a great deal.

Some time ago Richard said to me, "Mum, you need a new man in your life." I replied, "Not sure I am ready for one yet, Richard. What have you got in mind?" And quick as a flash he said, "One that likes rugby league so you have someone to keep you company at the games. I have Ashley." How funny it is that my son feels sorry for his poor old single mum! And then he said, "And someone that makes you laugh a lot. You like to laugh, Mum." Well, God has been amazingly kind and sent me someone truly special. He and Richard talk endlessly about sport, and he really, really makes me laugh—a lot. Wet-my-pants laugh a lot. Thanks, DV, for all you do, for all you say, for all your goodness, and for all your love. You are the best date I have ever had.

Richard, Richard . . . I am so proud of you, of who you are, how hard you try, how kind and loving you are to all you meet. You really are a beautiful soul. You are pure light and pure love. I love you a million, trillion, zillion. Thank you for being the best son ever. I am truly blessed.

And one last thing, as I think it is important to acknowledge companies that are prepared to make a difference, to take a risk, and to take action. The other day Rich and I went shopping. We love going to Kmart, and now I love going there even more, as greeting us as we walked in was a huge banner, big and bold and bright, and the smiling face looking back at us was a little boy with Down syndrome. Although we have a long way to go, there are retailers, businesses, and corporations that are grown-up enough to take the leap, embrace difference, and welcome inclusion. Thank you!

In Bob Dylan's immortal words, "The times they are a-changin.'"

## About the Author

Bernadette Agius has been the successful publisher of many self-help titles and is a trained mental health counselor. She is a fierce advocate for people with intellectual disabilities and believes their stories need to be told. Bernadette lives in Australia.